Beloved Strangers

Beloved Strangers

A Memoir

Maria Chaudhuri

BLOOMSBURY

NEW YORK • LONDON • NEW DELHI • SYDNEY

Published by Bloomsbury USA, New York
Bloomsbury is a trademark of Bloomsbury Publishing Plc

All papers used by Bloomsbury USA are natural, recyclable products made from wood grown in well-managed forests. The manufacturing processes conform to the environmental regulations of the country of origin.

LIBRARY OF CONGRESS CATALOGING-IN-PUBLICATION DATA

Chaudhuri, Maria.
Beloved strangers : a memoir / Maria Chaudhuri. — First U.S. edition.
pages cm
"First published in Great Britain in 2014"—Title page verso.
Includes bibliographical references and index.
ISBN: 978-1-62040-622-9 (hardback)
1. Chaudhuri, Maria. 2. Bangladeshi Americans—Biography. 3. Immigrants—United States—Biography. 4. Muslims—United States—Biography. 5. Young women—Biography. 6. Dhaka (Bangladesh) —Biography. 7. Jersey City (N.J.)
—Biography. 8. Coming of age. 9. Belonging (Social psychology) 10. Transnationalism—Psychological aspects. I. Title.
E184.B13C47 2014
305.8914'126073092—dc23
[B]
2013041951

First published in Great Britain in 2014
First U.S. Edition 2014

1 3 5 7 9 10 8 6 4 2

Typeset by Hewer Text UK Ltd, Edinburgh
Printed and bound in the U.S.A. by Thomson-Shore Inc., Dexter, Michigan

Bloomsbury books may be purchased for business or promotional use. For information on bulk purchases please contact Macmillan Corporate and Premium Sales Department at specialmarkets@macmillan.com.

To my father and mother: You are always with me.

To my brother and sisters: You are my laughter.

To my husband and son: You are my gifts.

'When you are sorrowful look again in your heart, and you shall see that in truth you are weeping for that which has been your delight.'

KAHLIL GIBRAN

Contents

Prologue

The Three Stages of Separation

Kicking and Screaming

Maybe the child already knew that once she stopped sharing the same body with her mother, her world would shatter irreparably. That knowledge alone must have made her cling to the walls of her mother's womb with all her infant strength.

Her mother lay on her back on a damp hospital bed, flanked on both sides by nurses in white. It was the hour after midnight, and she groaned with the pain of labour that had started eight hours ago. The sharpness had gone out of her cries. The only other sound was the unexpected December rain beating against the windows. And then, just as the nurses exchanged a tired look, neither mother nor child could hold on to each other any longer.

A great force overtook the two bodies that were still one, ripping them apart. Bones moving, skin splitting, tissues tearing. Blood, blood, more blood.

A head emerged, then a body, covered with the wounds of a perilous journey. As the nurse placed the baby in her mother's arms, the little one didn't cry, didn't make a single sound but, in the wake of separation, looked on with great surprise.

This was the story of my birth. My first separation. My disembodiment.

Learning to Fly

In one corner of our school playground there was a stack of red cement bricks piled high against a wall. The wall was low enough that if we climbed on top of the stack, we could peer over it into the neighbour's backyard. Every day when the last bell rang, my friend Nadia and I raced to the stack, climbed up on it and surveyed the view for a few minutes. It was not a spectacular backyard. The grass was not mown, the bushes were untended, and a child's broken crib lay discarded next to a rusty metal chair. But there was something enchanting about the garden. Tall stalks of wild lilies grew everywhere, giant roses burst forth from overgrown bushes and deliciously ripe red tomatoes rolled on the ground where someone had once made a vegetable patch. The image of that abandoned garden, mysterious, lonely, yet full of possibility, made my imagination soar.

'I want to run away,' I told my friend Nadia.

'Where to?'

'Dallas,' I said, remembering the Ewing family from the popular television show and their beautiful ranch in Dallas, Texas.

'Let's run away to New York! I have an uncle there.'

'So you'll come with me?'

'I could.'

We both remained silent for a moment, contemplating the feasibility of the plot.

'What about our parents?' I said at last.

Nadia frowned and I immediately regretted my query.

'They will forget about us,' she concluded with a slight twitch of her lips.

'You're right.' I agreed.

My friend nodded, linking her arm through mine. 'We could become actresses and get our own house. A big house with a red-tiled roof.'

'Or we could be detectives, like Nancy Drew and solve mysteries all the time.'

We looked at each other and giggled. We were inside our plot now – we were characters moving the plot forward. And we got into it so much that it became our daily after-school ritual in first grade. We spun the same reverie of escape and it left us breathless with excitement every time. Even as adults, we never really asked each other why, back then, it was so important for us to plan on running away.

It was not that home, for me, was an unhappy place. But in our home joy had an ephemeral quality to it. It was like trying to catch a glimmer of sunshine that slips in through a crack and dances around the room but never quite settles. We were novices at capturing joy, never able to hold on to it for very long.

I asked my mother one day what would make her truly happy. She thought for a second before responding, 'If I could go to a place very far away from here, all by myself, where I could just sing, I would be happy.'

My heart sank at the thought of losing Mother. 'Is there such a place?' I asked fearfully.

'Sure. Up in the mountains,' she replied.

I was young enough to think that avoiding mountains was the only way to keep Mother at home. But I was also old enough to understand that my mother was not happy at home. She needed to be up in the mountains to be happy. And she needed to be there alone. Despite myself, I began to devise subtle ways of leaving my mother alone. Perhaps if she could be left alone right *here* at home, she'd be happy and never leave for the mountains. So I listened to her more than I spoke to her. I observed her rather than follow her. I found ways to be near her without disturbing her. And I began to think that being alone was the right way to be. Even though it didn't always feel right. Especially when I had bad days at school and needed comfort and advice or when I struggled to understand something on my own but was too afraid to ask Mother about it or when I laid sick in bed wishing that someone would lie next to me and read me stories all night.

Letting Go

When I was eighteen years old, I left Dhaka and went to America to claim my new home. After that, Dhaka's trees, shrubs, air and water decided that I was not fit to return to her. So she attacked me and after she was done, the skin on my face was her burning red trophy, my sinuses and air passages the plundered pathways of her victory. She polluted her water so I could neither cool my infected organs nor douse the fire in my throat. I limped about the house, my whole body one large noxious pustule. My mother regarded me with dubious sympathy, 'But we are all breathing this air and drinking this water, and so did you for eighteen years!' How could I tell her that the water had been poisoned specially for my lips, the air made toxic only for my lungs? I knew what was happening to me was nothing but the seal of a vital separation between Dhaka and me, my old life and the new one I sought.

My older sister Naveen, who also returned to Dhaka for holidays, was never punished in the same way. The city greeted her with open arms, made her skin glow and rewarded her with hours of glorious rest and recreation. Naturally, my sister wanted me to snap out of it and join her in her sojourns. She too, regarded me with suspicion, 'Surely you can't be feeling *that* bad?'

Oh, but I did feel that bad. Even Dhaka's doctors were perplexed. It wasn't allergy season. The trees were almost bare. They couldn't figure out what was giving me this set of allergic reactions. One doctor asked, hopefully, if I ate a lot of shellfish. 'No,' I croaked, 'I don't eat any shellfish.' Another doctor suggested that we wash all the rugs and curtains in the house to get rid of mites. A tumultuous week followed. The maids scurried about, washing the curtains in boiling hot water. Rugs were cleaned and dried in the hot sun, floors were wiped with antiseptic solutions. The mites may have perished, but my misery lived on. The helpless doctors stuffed my eyes, ears, nose and mouth with every potion at their disposal until, finally, I lay in a limp and medicated heap, unable to move or speak. Still, the vile liquids flowed and flowed, draining my lymph system only to fill it to the brim again. They were viscous liquids of brilliant colours: crimson, green, yellow. Like wicked schools of fish they crawled along my body, spreading their venom everywhere.

The following year, I decided to arm myself with American ammunition to put up a fight against my Bengali ailment. Hidden under the layers of clothes and shoes in my suitcase, were my weapons – Claritin, Zyrtec, Allegra, Singulair, Nasonex, Benadryl, Sudafed, Tylenol-Sinus and many more. I anointed my body with the concoctions of war and waited for ambush. It came after three days of waiting. The liquids rose within me like an apocalypse. The war was over before it began. I lay in a state of semi-consciousness for days. The world came to me in shadows, moving closer in the shapes of hands that fed me more liquids. I dimly remember the desire for solidity and dryness. All I dreamed of during those melting hours was to be whole once more, to feel the entirety of my body, to be revitalised through every breath, to be held upright and propelled forward again by the force of each muscle, tissue, ligament and bone.

Each time I was there, Dhaka was merciless to me until she exiled me from her soil once more. As soon as my airplane lifted off Dhaka's angry bosom, my body would begin to repair itself. By the time I inhaled the frigid air of New York, I could smell again the rancid scents of coffee, fries and cigarettes. What had Dhaka smelled like? I longingly wondered. And I knew I would have to return to her, again and again, until my insides became redolent with her breath.

Saving Grace

I still remember the night my father came back from the hospital to tell me I'd had a baby sister instead of a baby brother. He tried to smile, but the muscles in his face wouldn't relax. In my five-year-old mind, I knew immediately what had gone wrong: I had cheated. Because I didn't understand Arabic I had translated my prayers into Bengali. But God must be spoken to in the Holy Language. I was too afraid to tell my father about my terrible mistake but it seemed that he already knew. He put me to bed and told me that the best time to ask for God's forgiveness was right before going to sleep, when the mind was too exhausted to lie.

I wasn't as eager for God's forgiveness as I was for my father's. It seemed that there was always a glass wall through which I viewed my father. This wall was my father's fear of God, his belief in what God wanted me to do rather than what he wanted from me. Every evening my father would come around to announce prayer time. He'd instruct me and my sister to perform our ablutions and go over the list of things to ask from God:

1. baby brother
2. long lives and good health
3. a big house of our own
4. a job at the World Bank head office in Washington D.C. for him.

My father warned us that if we didn't pray hard enough, God wouldn't answer us. I wanted to ask my father what would happen if God didn't answer our prayers but was afraid of upsetting him with such a question. We were supposed to believe in God because He was Merciful, Powerful and All-Knowing. We were supposed to believe that there was kindness in whatever He had in store for us, even if it caused suffering at times. If we believed in God, we had to have faith in His absolute knowledge. At five, I didn't understand God and His essence as well as I understood my need to please my father. I knew that if I tried to follow the instructions of God, I would please Father.

And so I imagined having God over for tea, getting to know Him over a light-hearted tête-à-tête. Would He drink his tea with milk and sugar, taking care to gingerly dip His Marie biscuits into the hot sweet liquid so as not to lose its crumbling edge inside the cup? Or, maybe we could invite Him for a real meal. Surely God would like the spicy mutton biryani and juicy haandi kebabs made by our cook Amol. Did God like to eat? He must. If He had never felt hunger in His life, how had He known to make us so hungry?

Ironically, my curiosity to know God was often frowned upon. Twice a week, Hujur, our Arabic tutor, came to teach us how to read the Holy Book. The Arabic words rolled along my tongue in an alluring tempo, inviting me to discover their meaning, but Hujur never explained the verses. When I dared to ask, he boxed my ears and said that the important thing was to recite the Holy Book in Arabic and to believe that every word in it was true.

'But I don't even know what I'm reading?'

'No questions,' he growled, 'just have faith.'

But I continued to ask Hujur questions. 'Where does God live?' I asked.

'He sits up there in Seventh Heaven, atop seven layers of sky,' replied Hujur.

'Does he ever come down from there?'

'He came down to the peak of Mount Surma once but his noor was so strong that the mountain burnt to ashes.'

'What is noor?'

'Noor is Light. Noor is Him. He has no form.'

'Then how do we know God is a He? It's just light, isn't it?'

'No more questions!'

I clapped a hand over my wretched mouth but it wouldn't stop.

Hujur mopped his brow with a cotton handkerchief, unable to quench my thirst for answers but he did try his best to instil the fear of God in me. He hoped, perhaps, that my fear would mitigate my curiosity.

To make sure that I was amply familiar with this aspect of fear, Hujur sang for me a special song. His song took pains to describe to me the images of Hell and Judgement Day. As his quavering, nasal voice rang out into the evening, I saw before my eyes great fires and devastating floods; naked human bodies being skinned alive and the sun, barely a foot above people's heads, melting their brains as they ran for their lives. If there was one thing Hujur did not tire of discussing, it was the wrath of God and the torture of Hell. That was the only time he willingly translated all the words from Arabic to Bengali.

I'm no longer sure whether it was the image of Hell or my desperation to please my father that urged me to kneel down and pray. I didn't always know what I was praying for but often it was for God's forgiveness. The winter I turned ten, I came to know of God's disdain for liars and it filled me with foreboding. Hujur came earlier than usual one evening. He had a thick black scarf wrapped around his neck but he looked cold in his white cotton tunic. He parked his rickety bicycle on our balcony and announced that he wanted to get back home before the fog came down hard.

'Caught a bad cold. Ask the cook to bring me some hot tea,' he said gruffly.

I was furious. I didn't care if he had pneumonia! All day I'd been waiting for the six o'clock WWF wrestling match. It promised to be a stunning battle. Big Daddy was going against Lex Luger. No one in my family understood why I loved these wrestling matches, I just did. I was thoroughly fascinated by those big, strong men, the precision of their fists, the friction of their bodies against each other, the wildness of their punches.

I cried helplessly as I washed myself with cold water and covered my hair with a scarf. My face was still dripping wet when I sat down in front of Hujur. I kept thinking of Lex Luger hurling his lithe body against Big Daddy's mountainous frame. I kept imagining the moment when Big Daddy would raise his towering girth, pick up Luger with his bare arms and twirl him above his head before throwing him out of the ring and on to the laps of screaming fans. Each new image brought fresh zeal to my whimpers until Hujur could no longer doze in peace and he held up a hand in an angry gesture.

'What is the matter with you, child?'

I stared at the floor.

'I asked you a question,' he repeated.

'Nothing, I'm fine,' I said meekly.

'You're lying. Why do you lie?'

'I'm not.'

'It's time you learned about the Angels of Death,' he said, shifting in his chair. 'After death, the two angels Munkar and Nakir come to visit the freshly deceased to test their faith. Whatever they ask, you must answer correctly. One small lie and those angels will make your grave grow smaller and smaller until the earth crushes your body so hard that even the mother's milk from your infant years will be squeezed out of you.'

I stopped whimpering.

'You see, child, if you lie in this life, you will lie in your grave,' said Hujur.

That night I dreamed of Munkar and Nakir. They were two ghastly little figures, dark and sleek with horned heads and hooves instead of feet. They had cloudy goat eyes. They grinned as they hopped from one grave to another until they found mine. I held my breath and burrowed deeper into the earth but they found me anyway.

'Do you believe in your Creator?' they asked in perfect unison.

'Yes.'

'Do you believe that He is your saviour?'

'Yes.'

'You lie,' they cackled. 'You lie, you lie.'

I lay there, unable to protest as the walls of my grave closed in on me from all sides. Just then, a thunderous noise bolted through the harrowing darkness. I saw Big Daddy scoop up the two scrawny angels in the palms of his giant hands and fling them across the expanse of the graves. They bounced off the stone edges of the old graves, yelping in pain to the brittle crunch of their bones. I tried to raise my body from my rapidly shrinking grave but it was too late. I only had time to look into Big Daddy's kind eyes for a moment before the earth squeezed in from above and below and flattened me to a pulp.

The next morning, I longed to tell my father about my dream. What did it mean? Was God going to punish me for all the small lies that had ever escaped my lips? My sister told me there was nothing wrong with white lies. For instance, if I felt upset and someone wanted to know why, I didn't have to tell them the real reason because it was my secret. The problem was, I didn't always know how to differentiate between a white lie and a real one.

I fiddled with my toast and kept my brimming eyes on the table, hopeful that my father would notice my silence and ask me what was wrong. He never looked up from his newspaper. In the end, I decided not to tell my father about the dream or my fear of being punished for all the lies I had ever uttered. I knew what would please him more was if I just knelt before God and asked for His forgiveness.

There were, nevertheless, some people who were close to God in ways that the rest of us could never hope to be. The pir sahib, for instance – the old man with an uncomfortably long beard who came to our house every year. My father and mother would rush to the door and kneel at his feet, nudging me to do the same. My father explained that he was a holy man with special powers. Try as I might, I couldn't bring myself to perceive this singular camaraderie between the pir and the Almighty. What I saw was a gnarled old man whose eyes preyed on his surroundings like a hungry animal on the prowl. I sensed a deep rumbling inside him, like the earth heaving before an earthquake.

Every time I went near the pir sahib he tried to catch hold of my hand and asked me to scratch his back. He would shout out my name and claim that he had a story to tell me about my namesake, a certain Maria al Qibtiya of Egypt.

'Come to me, my little one,' he'd repeat incessantly. 'Let me tell you a story about your name.'

I'd try to hide behind my mother but she would push me forward until I fell at his feet, touching withered yellow skin, for blessings divine. The pir's words, his touch, his very presence would heal me, my mother said. Heal me from what?

Everyone around me seemed to be in dire need of healing. While the pir slept through the long afternoons, hordes of people poured into our small home in the hope of touching his yellow feet for a split second, to heal their wounded souls. Men and women of all ages, ayahs carrying crying toddlers on their hips and little girls and boys dressed in their best, packed themselves like canned sardines into our living room, spilling out of our kitchen and veranda. They waited tirelessly, their reveries of divine awakening broken only by the tinkling of china as Amol served them cup after cup of lukewarm tea.

Only when the dusty curve of the afternoon had bent around an orange dusk would the pir wake to sit up on his bed and bellow, 'Bring me hot water for my wazoo.' And right there, in our living room, a stampede would break out. A multitude of bodies would compete for the task of fetching water to wash the old man's blessed limbs and prepare him for an exclusive communion with God. As the entire house full of people bustled to join the pir for evening prayer, I'd run up to the coolness of the roof and stare hard at the pink evening sky. My grandmother said it was in the moment between twilight and darkness that all heavenly creatures left their earthly sojourns to fly back up to the heavens. The pink streaks in the sky were Heaven's doorways, flung open for the return of its inhabitants.

I was always hunted down before the multi-coloured easel of a sky had coagulated into a deep charcoal. Despite all protests, I was always dragged downstairs for the communal prayer.

No one really knew if the pir learned about the future from those long one-on-one communions with God or whether he was born with his powers. But no one doubted him when he assured my mother that her third child would be a boy.

'Sister, your time has come to bear your husband a boy. I can see it with my eyes open.'

He tied a special talisman around my mother's neck, a square silver amulet hung from a black string that she wore for nine months. She also drank three drops of holy water every day from a bottle that he sealed with a special prayer. No one was allowed to drink from that bottle except my mother. A few weeks before she was due to give birth, the pir sahib touched her belly, muttered something and blew on it, his saintly breath pledging the imminent arrival of a boy.

So when my little sister kicked her way into the world, a wobbly seven pounds of female flesh, there was only a boy's name waiting for her. After three days had passed and there was still no name for the little girl, my grandmother named her Tilat. The pir came to our house to bless the baby and my mother confronted him with an ominous silence.

'Don't look at me like that, sister,' he said. 'God changed his mind at the last minute. I saw it happen. Did you go to another pir?'

'Of course not,' she protested.

'Think,' he urged. 'Think hard.'

My mother stayed up all night, thinking about how she might have jeopardised the pir's charms. At last it came to her. In the final weeks of her pregnancy, she had found an old almanac among her grandmother's things, a useful handbook that contained specific prayers for specific situations. Hours had passed as she read about which verses to chant to cure an adulterous husband and which to recite in case of a fire. There was nothing that couldn't be warded off or heralded by the power of the holy verses. There were prayers for each and every problem. Then she found it, in bold letters, the prayer that would hail the birth of a baby boy. Why not add it to her repertoire of prayers, she thought.

When she told the pir about her little transgression, he was livid.

'Well, that's it!' he said, 'I knew you had done something to diffuse the effect of my methods. Did you not have enough faith in me?'

'I did,' my mother sobbed. 'I just didn't see the harm in repeating one more prayer.'

'You silly woman,' squawked the pir. 'Haven't you ever heard of the saying that too many cooks spoil the broth?'

While my mother howled, I made a mental note to myself not to pester God beyond a reasonable limit. I would make my request to Him and then I would leave Him alone. He was a busy man. If I made unfair demands on His time, maybe I would have more to lose than to gain.

The mishap of my baby sister's birth thus explained, the pir sahib continued to visit us with his probing eyes and empty promises for the future. I managed to stay out of his way until one sweltering hot afternoon when his gaze firmly settled on me. He had dozed off after lunch and my parents had gone to buy some fish for dinner. The pir liked fish. He gobbled up whole pieces of fish, including the bones, and bared his crooked dentures afterwards in a gesture of triumph. He dipped fish heads into soupy daal and slurped at them surreptitiously, letting the yellow liquid stain his white beard.

I didn't want to be left alone with him. I had pleaded with my mother to take me with them but she felt that the fish market was no place for a child. Besides, what if the pir needed something?

No sooner had my parents left than the pir started shouting my name. There was an urgency in his voice, a sharpness. Had he really been sleeping? Even as I walked over to him, I debated if I should pretend not to hear him. I reached his bed and looked down at him. He peered up at me through his ancient eyes, thin slits under a white canopy of eyebrows. His long white hair lay in limp strands on the pillow.

'Do you need something?' I asked.

'Sit,' he said, patting the bed. 'I have a story to tell you.'

It was the story he had been trying to tell me for years, the story of my namesake that defined me in his eyes. I didn't want to hear it. But he had insisted for so long now. Would he leave me alone if I let him tell me the story once and for all? I sat down. He looked pleased and cupped my hands in his. They were unusually warm.

'How old are you, child?'

'I'm almost twelve,' I said.

'Ah, almost a woman.'

I didn't respond.

'Did your mother tell you that I named you?'

'Yes,' I said.

'Do you know where your name comes from?'

'No.'

'Well, it's time you knew. I named you after a beautiful woman called Maria al Qibtiyya. She was a Christian slave, gifted to the Prophet by the Byzantine Emperor. He was enthralled by her beauty. He married her and she bore him a son.'

He paused and stared at me. 'Do you know why I named you after her?'

'No,' I said.

'Because you're beautiful, just like her. All women are made beautiful. Do you understand?'

'Yes,' I said, although I didn't really understand his point.

'Smart girl,' he said.

He paused again, tightening his hands around mine.

I remember the silence and a certain heightening of my senses. I remember noticing his tongue, slightly protruding between his lips, as he studied my face. I remember smelling a strange fleshy odour and wondering where it came from. I remember that the moments passed quickly yet painstakingly, derailing my sense of time. I remember his hands wrapping

17

around mine like tight, cold snakes. I remember the sound of my parents' car pulling into the driveway, breaking the silence that was so terribly loud. I remember feeling the urge to urinate.

I ran to the window and watched my parents emerge with clear water-filled plastic bags full of fresh fish, alive and wriggling.

'Did he wake up? Did he need anything?' my mother asked anxiously.

'He didn't need anything,' I said slowly.

She looked at me then, and just for a moment, she held my gaze. Then she looked away.

'Your father will want you to wash up for evening prayers. Hurry up.'

My father was the last person I wanted to see right then. I knew I would be admonished later for not joining the prayers, but for now, I needed to hide from my parents and their beloved pir sahib.

I went to the kitchen and watched the fish flailing in the sink where Amol had dumped them. I wondered how long it would be before the air was depleted from their lungs rendering their little bodies limp and lifeless.

The month of Ramzan, which follows the cycle of a new moon, appeared at slightly different times each year. During the holy month of Ramzan, explained my father, we were to pledge our allegiance to God by fasting from dawn to dusk, cleansing ourselves of our deepest desire, the desire to eat and therefore perhaps to live. At the end of the day, we could rejuvenate ourselves by celebrating the very desire we renounced all day. I see now a blurry logic in the simultaneous renouncement and celebration of life; a roundabout attempt to affirm the entirety of the life-and-death cycle by invoking them in turn.

The year I turned fifteen, Ramzan fell in July, the hottest month of the year. School was out but there was no escape from the blistering heat. When we woke to eat sehri, the pre-dawn meal, Amol would place pitcher after pitcher of ice cold water on the table, which vanished before he had a chance to turn his back. The old ceiling fan blew nothing but hot air and even the mosquitoes were too sluggish to drink our salt-drained blood. In that heat, it was impossible to digest Amol's flaming curries and sizzling grilled meats, so my mother poured cold milk over our rice and threw in chopped bananas to make a sticky mixture. Sitting in the semi-darkness, with our assortment of sweet milk-and-banana rice, curries, kebabs and ghee-soaked parathas, my family devoutly prepared for the day ahead. As soon as the sun started to appear in the eastern sky, illuminating the shapes of trees and buildings, I'd desperately try to gulp down one last glass of water.

'Hurry,' my mother often prompted. 'When the maulana starts the morning prayer call you have to stop eating and drinking.'

'Nonsense,' my grandmother snapped. 'It's not the prayer call that matters. As long as there isn't enough light to see the hair on your own body, you can keep eating.'

It made me wonder about those who did not have enough body hair to begin with. My grandmother had practically hairless limbs, making her sip her second cup of tea as calmly as a Buddha, while the rest of us scrambled to finish our meals.

Something happened to me that year. Something dislodged and broke away somewhere deep inside my cells, leaving a gluttonous, gaping hole. It left me breathless and impatient. It left me standing in the midday sun, throwing stones at the crows that came to scrounge scraps of food from the small veranda next to the kitchen. Sweat stuck to my skin and clothes like honey, leaving me so parched I felt I could drink water out of a toilet bowl. I found myself walking to the kitchen every so often to get a whiff of iftar, the delectable evening meal that Amol prepared for the breaking of fast. My mind kept whirring around the images of spicy red daal marinated and fried to crispiness, black peas curried with onions and tomatoes and the delicious caramely Mecca dates, imported specially for Ramzan. Being Christian, Amol didn't observe Ramzan, and I hovered around him, finding twisted consolation in watching him eat his meals: breakfast of sugared milk with thickly buttered chapatti; for lunch, generous portions of fried fish, rice and fresh cool salads of coriander, tomatoes and cucumber.

During Ramzan, my father usually came home early from work. He'd stack his briefcase neatly under his desk, change into a clean white kurta, place a white topi on his head and quietly settle into his favourite chair, prayer beads in hand. I was disconcerted by the serenity he exuded, the stillness in his posture. How could he look so content when all I could do was count the seconds till I dowsed the fire in my belly?

To make matters worse, the terrible pangs of hunger were followed by terrible pangs of guilt. The whole point of fasting was to conquer the throes of hunger and desire and every time I groaned or complained or thought about food, I fell from God's grace. So I gritted my teeth and plodded through the day, because, Heaven forbid, if I made my feelings known, I would fall from my father's grace as well.

The desperate attempt to distract myself from my all-consuming hunger, led me, one intolerable afternoon, to pick up the phone and call my friend Raqib. Half an hour later, we were sitting on the rooftop, gazing unsurely at the street below. I had always liked him but why had I sought his company just then and why had he complied so easily? Thoughts bubbled up to our lips but starvation left us too exhausted to speak. In truth, words were useless. I clasped his hand in mine, more out of frustration than anything else.

At the touch, our hunger flowed out of us with volcanic rage, sweeping everything else out of our way. Our bodies were so clammy we could barely slide our hands over each other's skin but we clung to each other. Our kiss was deep and voracious but also inexpert and unexciting. It was not a kiss that was born out of love or lust. It was a kiss born out of starvation and frustration. And yet we knew that fasting was supposed to give us a sense of spiritual fulfilment and purpose that would help us rise above the physical hardship of the feat. So where was it, that restorative feeling of salvation at the end of every blood-draining fast? I waited for it every day and when it didn't come, I tried to find it through that kiss, an act of defiance, a silent mutiny. I had hoped that by violating the rules of a fast (through engaging in any form of physical union), I could at least guilt my way back to being an unquestioning believer in its worth.

But, at the end of the long kiss, I was surprised by the rush of relief that swept over of me. It was as if a high fever had broken and, along with it, my delirium. By breaking the divinely ordained rules of fasting, I had unleashed a profound hunger, one that neither food nor flesh could satisfy. I began to understand that it was precisely this kind of hunger – this corroding, corrupting hunger, a hunger that turned us into untamed, untethered creatures – that we were meant to curb and conquer. Through fasting.

Despite the sanctioned celebration of all those fleshy delights – the kebabs and grills and stews for sehri and iftar and countless other occasions, such as the naming ceremony of a newborn or the odd animal sacrifice to ward off a forthcoming misfortune, my mother just couldn't make me eat enough meat. I wanted white jasmine rice, potatoes in red jackets, the golden soup of slow-cooked lentils, the long green bodies of lady's fingers and green beans, the fiery red of tomatoes and the purple of eggplants. I could not bear to look at the sinewy masses of flesh floating in Amol's curries. When I ate meat every bit of me became aware of the distinct textures of bone, muscle and cartilage. The first time I saw the heart of a chicken, I stared at the caricature of the human heart, noticing that the slender pipe-like ventricle that separated the atria connected the chambers in much the same manner as mine. Later, I was served the same heart, its slippery consistency singed into a congealed mass that no longer quivered. In fact, we had intimate knowledge of not only the bird's unfortunate heart but also of its gizzard, its liver and other bits of the gastrointestinal tract that I do not care to recall.

'Eat,' my mother said, if we put up the slightest resistance. 'I don't have time for any nonsense.'

'Spoiled children,' my grandmother added. 'Do you know how many kids in this country starve every day?'

Hers was a curious logic. Poor kids could not eat so rich kids should eat everything in sight. Nonetheless, on the morning when I witnessed the Great Sacrifice, I did see for myself the desperation in the eyes of those scrawny, hungry children.

The sounds of preparation woke me early: steel knives sharpening against stone blocks, the clang of pots and pans and the chop chop chop of onions and garlic. Through the gap in my curtains, I saw the woman next door arranging young, green banana leaves on the floor of her balcony. I heard the plaintive bleating of animals held captive by an entire city of devotees. It was the day of Eid-ul-Adha, the day on which Abraham sacrificed his son to prove his love for God. The world changed thereafter, for sheep and cattle anyway, as humankind was led, by example, to perform the supreme sacrifice that kept their sons at home but still managed to please God.

By the time I showed up in my new Eid dress, the men had neatly divided into two groups of starched white soldiers. My father and uncles were issuing orders and instructions, while the cook and the butchers were bustling around with the tools of their trade. The cows had been brought from the stinking shed in the backyard. One of the young calves nestled against his mother while the other squatted, head reclined feverishly. Their mother stood calmly. One of the men followed my gaze. 'Hello, little missy, you like? Very tender meat,' he grinned. 'Good for seekh kebab.'

Then it was time. The buzz of conversation died, everyone got into position. The head-butcher stepped forward with a long curved knife while four men circled the mother cow. In one imperceptible, lightning motion, they threw her down on the damp ground and flipped her on her back. She laid there, belly up, surprised, as they expertly tied all four of her legs together. She seemed to resist but only for one jerking, joking second.

'In the name of God,' chanted a chorus of voices as the gleaming machete came down on the soft skin of her throat.

I peered into her dying eyes that had turned skywards and I saw the life seeping out of them. A fountain of blood sprouted from her neck and I sensed the warmth bubbling out of her body. A final guttural groan was wrenched from deep within her and splashed across the humid morning. Red betel juice dripped from the corners of the machete man's mouth and trickled slowly down his chin.

I watched as she turned into a limpid pool of redness, a mountain of white bones. They spread her out on banana leaves, skin, head, limbs and torso. Her eyes were glassy but her jaws were parted with slight deliberation. It was the hint of a smile, a smile that gave her the dignity to rise above her massacred body.

The hordes of children started to arrive with their empty gunny sacks. They approached boldly and climbed up the rusted iron grille of the old gate like little monkeys. It did not shock me that they awaited their day's meal with pleasure. What unsettled me was the look in their eyes, the way they stared at the kill, with the grim satisfaction of those who could only understand the meaning of blood in the context of spilling it. What fast could curb such appetite, tame such impulsion?

The butcher was heading towards the squatting calf. I turned around and started to run back to the house.

'Hey you,' yelled someone. 'Don't be such a sissy.'

I kept running. Behind me I heard the voices rise again as they prepared to slaughter the calf. Just as I reached the threshold of our porch, I turned back to look at my father. But he had his back to me. Had he even noticed me slip away? Or was he too disappointed to acknowledge my cowardice?

The sight of the catfish wiggling in the shallow green pool of water in front of Shah Jalal Baba's shrine filled me with foreboding because my father told me they were not real fish. In 1303, when Shah Jalal, the great saint from Delhi, came to Bengal to preach Islam, he defeated the ruling Hindu king, Gour Gobinda. Deeming that many of the king's followers practised witchcraft, he turned them into catfish, condemning them as eternal examples of those who stray from the true path of God. Through centuries, these human-catfishes continued to live, their souls trapped in ugly black bodies, their bodies kept in a filthy tank for display.

Inside the prayer hall of the mausoleum, I could not concentrate on the prayers I was supposed to recite in order to pay respect to the saint's departed soul. I made frequent mistakes, disturbed by the vision of a family of catfish, roaming in unending agony. Around me, women prayed in various states of fervour. Some sat in rigid meditation, eyes closed, fingers nimbly moving through prayer beads. Others beat their foreheads on the hard ground, crying for mercy, pleading for the redemption of their sinful souls.

After the prayers, Mother, Naveen, Tilat and I waited for my father and Avi to come down from the elevated section of the mausoleum where the men prayed. I would have given anything to enter the demarcated area containing the actual tomb of the saint, to kneel at his feet and beg for forgiveness on behalf of the old catfishes. But Shah Jalal Baba did not permit women to go near his tomb.

'If I go near his tomb, will he turn me into a catfish too?' I asked my mother.

'Don't be silly. And try to keep your head covered for as long as you're here,' she said, adjusting the long scarf wrapped around my small head.

Visiting the crypt of Shah Jalal Baba was one of the three reasons that my parents planned a family trip to Sylhet every winter. The pir lived in Sylhet too and my father loved to visit him, showering his brood of snot-nosed children with our old clothes and toys, bringing him generous gifts of food and money. The pir never refused. Being a man of God, he preferred to live on alms. For long hours during those trips, Naveen, Tilat, Avi and I would wander aimlessly in the pir's ramshackle backyard while my parents, along with his other disciples, laid their offerings at his feet and vied for his attention.

Not that my father ever spoke of it, but one of the reasons for visiting Sylhet was also my father's secret desire to introduce us to the place of his childhood, a desire that he could not voice, given his reticence. Occasionally, we grasped his attachment to the streets and bazaars of Sylhet when he pointed out to us, with great pride, the sweetmeat shop selling the freshest jilapis or the streetside restaurant serving the best pickled bitter gourd. One time, he showed us a low white building, atop a hill, which had been his high school. We asked him if we could visit the school grounds but he firmly shook his head. Other times, unable to contain his excitement at a sudden sight or smell, my father would start jabbering in the local Sylheti dialect, something he only used when talking to the locals. On realising his slip, he would quickly retreat into his characteristic silence. What he was unable to share hung between us like the winter fog that shrouded the old town in secrecy.

For me, the best parts of those annual trips came in the early morning and late night hours. We always stayed at an old inn called Bagh Bari. Even though the inn was technically in Sylhet town, in reality, it seemed to be in the middle of nowhere. Our wobbly, rented microbus veered off the main road and followed a narrow vein of pathways for at least a half hour before we reached Bagh Bari, which stood amidst rolling hills extending on all sides. No other habitation seemed to be in sight so that when we peered out of the window at night, there was only pitch darkness. Legend had it that Bagh Bari, which literally meant Tiger House, was once flanked by deep forests where Bengal Tigers ambled with royal ease at all times of the day, until finally, the inhabitants of Bagh Bari abandoned their perilous home and left for ever.

In truth, Bagh Bari still looked like an ancient, abandoned home. Dust caked the window seals, the furniture groaned and creaked and the sheets smelled musty. There was no hot water but the heavyset innkeeper, Dowla Babu, would bring us boiling water for our baths in rusty iron buckets. There never seemed to be other guests in the inn, either. But my siblings and I didn't care. We loved that our parents always got the largest room in the inn so we could all stay together. At night, when we returned to Bagh Bari, after a day of prayers and blessings and trying to find God, we finally got a taste of the fun and freedom that all children long for. Mother let us take long baths with the iron bucketfuls of hot water and as we engaged in delightful water fights, she hummed and leaned back against the pillows, while, next to her, Father peacefully read his newspaper. Through the half open bathroom door, we could see them, their reposed forms a reminder that the confusing day had come to an end and we could relax now. After dinner, Naveen, Tilat, Avi and I rolled around on the extra mattress on the floor, which had been lugged in for us, our minds churning with images of holy men, magic fish, divine-smelling sweetshops, Bengal Tigers and our father as a young boy, until we drifted off to the lilting sound of our parents' soft voices above us.

In the mornings, Dowla Babu knocked on our door because breakfast was at 7 a.m. sharp. Sunlight swaddled the small dining room, where we sat at a table piled high with plates of omelettes and toast. A jar of orange marmalade and a dish of butter rested next to a big pot of tea. These were the only times Father spread butter and jam on our toast and cut the eggs into small pieces for Tilat and Avi. As an additional treat, Mother poured small amounts of overmilky tea into pink and white teacups for Naveen and me. We didn't want breakfast to end, didn't want to get into the dreadful microbus, didn't want to go to the pir's dingy house full of haunted-looking children, didn't want to pray at any saint's tomb. We wanted to stay right there in Bagh Bari, play with Dowla Babu's big brown cat Bagha, run along the slopes of the rolling hills, hear stories of our father's childhood in that very town, listen to Mother hum a happy tune.

It isn't until years later, long after my father is no longer alive to preach the benefits of his faith – his unshakeable faith – that it lays a hand on my shoulder to tell me with a certainty I'd once seen in my father's eyes, that all is not lost; that there is a way out.

The bazaar at Banani is a veritable war zone of fruitsellers and fishmongers and overzealous chicken vendors who walk up to customers to shove a bunch of squawking feathers in their unsuspecting faces. On any given day, if you walk through the bazaar, you are unlikely to avoid stepping on a sopping mess of rotten fruit, fish goop and chicken shit. What you may not notice, however, is a narrow flight of broken stairs, almost fully hidden behind the jumble of fruit and fish stalls.

I make my way up the small flight of stairs, slick with mud and rain, nearly stepping on a half-eaten apple molested by flies. The stairs lead up to a narrow corridor with three closed doors. The first one says: 'Homeopathy. Skin Disease. All Types of Diseese OK.' The second door says nothing but bears four marks from where a sign had once hung. The third door says 'Kazi. Registrar of Marriage. Banani.' I take a deep breath before knocking on the third door.

'Come in,' says a man's voice.

The kazi sits behind a wooden desk stacked high with paper files. He is wearing an ankle-length tunic of light grey cotton and a white skullcap which resembles a yarmulke. I notice the rosary beads wrapped around his wrist as he strokes his long henna-stained beard. I know kazis are empowered by the Islamic law of the state to conduct and dissolve marriages. But sitting behind that mountain of lives built and broken on paper, meeting those eyes that steadily held my faltering ones, I feel that the man before me is larger than the jurisdiction of the law. I notice two other men sitting on wooden chairs at the other end of the room who look like younger versions of the kazi.

'How can I help you?' the kazi asks in a booming voice.

'I need to file for a divorce.'

The two men sit up straighter. The kazi looks undeterred. 'Where is your guardian?'

'I don't have one. I am an adult.'

'Where is your father?' he asks, raising an eyebrow.

'My father has passed away.'

'Mother?'

'I think we need to talk about my divorce.'

The younger men sniggered, all the while busily scanning my entire form.

'What are your grounds?' The kazi asks, his tone now decidedly stern.

'My husband and I don't get along. He is emotionally abusive.'

'What do you mean by that?'

'Well, he gets very angry and paranoid.'

'Does he beat you?'

'No, but—'

'Then what are your grounds?'

'I told you. He abuses me mentally.'

'Does he use swear words?'

'Not really.'

'Does he have relations with other women?'

'I don't think so.'

'Then I am failing to see your grounds.'

'He yells and shouts for no reason. He gets depressed and doesn't talk to me for days and he lies to me about every single thing.'

'What kind of lies?'

'He lied about his birth, his age. He even lied about his nationality.'

Despite myself I cannot help but imagine my spouse's fate at the hands of the angels of death.

The kazi fondles his beard, 'Why does he lie? Is he angry with you for some reason?'

'He's angry at the whole world, not just me.'

The kazi shakes his head slowly as he speaks. 'Lying is not right but that is not a good enough reason to divorce him. It is a wife's duty to understand the motives of her husband. Why don't you come back with him and maybe things will be clearer to me.'

Since Hujur's description of a liar's punishment, no one had bothered to tell me that lying can be acceptable under certain situations. 'How am I to understand him? He doesn't even talk to me!' I cry.

Through the open window of the small office, the rank smell of fish and fowl drifts in. The men fidget in their chairs. They are beginning to lose interest in me. I need them to look at me, acknowledge me, listen to me. Yet, I cannot beg and plead – my dignity bars that path. I cannot possibly lean across the table and say with any desirable impact, 'You really have no idea what you're talking about.' In fact, I cannot find a suitable way to talk to these men, though I share race and nation with them. We face each other across completely unknown ground, their indifference matching my discomfort. We search for common ground. We need to agree on something, anything.

'Look,' I say, 'I can give you a very good reason for filing this divorce.'

'Then give it to me,' comes the impatient reply.

'He's an alcoholic. My husband is an incurable alcoholic. He is always drunk and I cannot imagine that he will sober up long enough to agree to this divorce, let alone turn up for it.'

And there it is, the secret of my marriage that riles the men of faith. All three of them look at me as if for the first time and nod sympathetically, disapproval dawning on their faces. The kazi reaches for a stack of forms on his desk.

'Fill this out,' he says softly. 'Religion does not stipulate you to live with an alcoholic. Remember, your faith comes before your marriage.'

As I make my way out of Banani Bazaar, child vendors selling brooms and kitchen rags following closely at my heels, I think about what Father would have done in my situation. Had he regarded marriage as an institution of God, the love in it born and bred as per God's rules? Or might he have agreed with me that the only God in a marriage between two people was created by their love?

My grandmother taught me a special prayer for protection when the fear of ghosts and spirits kept me awake at night. This prayer, when summoned in true faith, possessed the ability to cleanse, purify and protect everything that came into close contact with its very sound and tremor. Nanu instructed me to recite the prayer, blow into my cupped hands with my instantly-purified breath and clap three times as loudly as possible. As far as the sound of the clapping reached, all evil energies would be immediately banished. No matter who recited it or what situation called for it, this prayer effectively invoked the Supreme and banished the existence of all that contradicted it.

'Whatever you do,' Nanu advised, 'don't ever forget this verse and God will always protect you.'

It must have been extra hot that summer, to make us sleep with the windows open while the ceiling fan spun in full blast. I shared a room with Tilat and our two-year-old brother Avi.

There was one double bed, which Tilat and Avi slept on, and one single bed, which was mine. I am not sure how long the sound had been going on but by the time it penetrated my brain deeply enough to wake me up, it had become pretty loud. It was an odd rattling noise intermittently interrupted by the sound of hammering. My eyes immediately flew to the other bed and locked in with Tilat's wide open, terror-filled ones. How long had she been awake?

Something told me not to speak out loud or turn my head towards the window where the noise was coming from. Instead, I squeezed my eyes shut and uttered the prayer that Nanu had taught me. After reciting the prayer a few times and fortifying the room with its powers, I bolted upright in bed and hissed at Tilat to grab Avi and run to our parents' room. Tilat must have been holding her breath for an instruction from me. In one scoop, she picked up our sleeping brother and fled towards the door. Even though I still did not dare to look at whatever was at the window, I could hear the strange commotion come to an abrupt halt. I tensed my body for whatever was to come and shouted at Tilat to run as fast as she could.

Just as Tilat opened the door to our room, an astonishing thing happened. A flood of light streamed in from the corridor outside where my father stood, looking rather astounded. Tilat screeched, and I, finding the courage now, quickly turned to look at the window, only to catch a fleeting shadow moving away.

'What on earth is going on here?' my father asked, stepping into our room and switching on the light.

He followed my gaze and in the bright light all our eyes widened to see the cracked and broken section of the window grille that the burglar had been trying to hack away, presumably with a hammer. He must have used a ladder to get up on the ledge right under the window from where he stood and tried to undertake his very unfurtive operation. Not that we felt any less shaken by the whole episode, but the thief was clearly a person of little intelligence. In fact, the more we discussed it the next day, the more we were intrigued and entertained by the sheer folly of his ingenuous plan. Even if he had somehow managed not to wake us with his pandemonium, how on earth was he planning to squeeze through a small grille-less portion of the window? In the days to come, our favourite game was playing 'burglar burglar' by reenacting that night's series of events. Even little Avi cackled every time Tilat banged on the window with a pretend hammer made out of a pencil box.

But one thing remained unsolved despite the comicality of the night's affairs. How had my father turned up at the exact moment we sought him?

'Did you hear a noise? Is that why you came to our room?' I asked him.

'I didn't hear any noise,' he said matter-of-factly. 'I had a strange dream. And when I woke up I felt I needed to check on you kids.'

I found it impossible to believe that my father had been woken by a dream at the same moment when I was instructing Tilat to fetch my parents.

'What did you dream?' I asked, hesitantly.

'Doesn't matter,' he said gruffly.

'I asked Tilat to run to your room when I heard the noise but before she reached you, you magically appeared!' I confessed, overwhelmed with awe and gratitude. I wanted nothing more than to bury my head in my father's chest and have him tell me that he would always be there when I needed him.

'There is no magic, dear,' Father said calmly. 'Only God.'

'Yes, but—'

'Did you say your prayers before bed?'

'Yes and also when I heard the noise.'

'See? It was God who protected you. I was merely an excuse. And if I hadn't been there, you would have found another way out of it.'

I lowered my head, not wanting to hear any more. Not because I didn't want God's protection. But because I was losing, for the millionth time in my childhood, the chance to see my father as my protector, my hero. In my father's denial of his personhood, of his role as my guiding star, there was the gallant notion that he had placed me in the care of a Supreme Custodian, whose guardianship was matched by none.

'Oh, and you should always bolt the windows at night,' he added after a moment's thought.

There was nothing more to be said. In my father's system-atised universe, there was no place for parental intuition, reassuring fatherly embraces or even a child's wonder. He was always careful not to reach down and touch me or sit me on his lap or explain anything beyond the necessary, lest he shatter the glass wall through which I saw him, every day. In his mind, he didn't need to do any of those things. Ultimately, we were all the children of God and, as an earthly parent, my father's only duty was to guide us towards our *real*, heavenly Father.

Fallen

I learned the word 'shame' in kindergarten. Mrs Lohani, with the triangular face and the huge mole on her nose, administered the word to me. If we became too rowdy in class, she banged her wooden desk loudly with the blackboard duster, wrinkled her nose and chirped 'shame-shame' in a sing-song voice. 'You are big boys and girls now. How can you be so loud and unruly? Shame-shame,' she'd say. Thus, shame came into my life with its twin, shame.

Mrs Bashir, my first-grade maths teacher, continued the task of shaming me. I struggled in her class the most. My mind muddled over additions and subtractions; it divided when asked to multiply. The morphology of numbers was lost on me – why did they have to come together only to transform into something else? Mrs Bashir's small and wriggly handwriting made the numbers look like little white worms inching their way up the blackboard. She regarded us sternly, proclaiming every day, even when we were quiet and peaceful, what an unruly, spoiled group of children we were. I found myself look-ing out of the window and daydreaming as soon as Mrs Bashir walked into class. Invariably, Mrs Bashir would fling my lesson book across the classroom, grab me by both ears to pick me up and place me, red-faced and burning, on the 'shaming bench' outside the classroom. There I remained until the noonday sun baked my skin dry. As the energy seeped out of me in streams of sweat, it took all my strength not to faint.

The shaming continued until it became clear that I would not make the same mistakes again. I stopped making mistakes because I stopped being able to add or subtract at all. On one occasion, Mrs Bashir was perplexed when she opened my lesson book to see that I'd neatly copied the assignment but left it entirely undone. Concluding that the shaming had been inadequate, she dragged the red bench, which had stood just outside the classroom window, inside, and placed it next to the teacher's desk so the victim could squarely face the gleeful spectators of her torture. Saved from the tropical sun, my skin began to recover its natural tone again but my six-year-old heart was broken. As my classmates looked on mockingly, I hung my head and wished I would faint after all.

At the time, I didn't wonder why Mrs Bashir simply didn't inform my mother of my numerical deficiencies. It would have been quite natural for her to inform my parents, given that rigorous punishment had not cured me of my shortcomings. Except that the same fact also made her prickle with indigna-tion, suggesting her methods had failed. Gritting her teeth, she boxed my ears extra hard one day and accused me of feigning innocence. 'You devious, lazy child,' she shrieked, 'I know what you're doing. You'd rather stand in the sun than do your work, so you pretend you can't do it. And you think I will eventually take pity on you and stop the punishment? Well, I won't!'

If Mrs Bashir had been intolerant of my mathematical weaknesses, she was livid at the thought of my slyness. Every single day, for the span of the school year, I was a circus freak, hauled up to the red bench for an open exhibit of my deformities. My ears were always red, either from the constant grabbing and twisting or from the constant shame I felt.

That was when I invented the odd game with numbers. I ran up and down the shapes of their horrid bodies, hid in their nooks and crannies and refused to hear anything they might have to say to me. I fantasised chopping them into edible bits and gobbling them up, once and for all, so they'd leave me alone. No matter what I tried though, they stayed with me. They greeted me every morning from the pages of my books, cooing incessantly in my head, 'Shame-shame, shame-shame, shame-shame . . .'

Once I understood shame – a lesson that had begun with my attempt to understand God – I realised that it was all around me, either trying to hide, or waiting to be noticed. There was Lima, for example, who suddenly turned up at our doorstep one day with amber eyes full of mortification. Uncle Karim, my mother's youngest brother, brought Lima to our home. As soon as they came, my uncle took my mother aside and whispered something in her ear. I saw my mother's eyes soften as she greeted Lima and took her hand in hers and I sensed that something of an alliance was formed. It was different from the way she greeted a regular guest. Lima started visiting us daily with her eight-year-old daughter Faiza, who was the same age as me. In the beginning, Lima sat in our living room, sipped lemon tea from gold-rimmed bone-china cups and spoke to my mother in hushed tones. I was asked to play with Faiza. My heart remained in the unheard conversations of the adults. I knew it would not be long before my mother would repeat the story to my father or grandmother, simply overlooking my presence. Adults, it seemed to me, were punctilious with ceremony but artless when it came to strategy.

As anticipated, Lima's story was revealed one Sunday in the environment of domestic chit-chat, exempt of censorship. It turned out that Lima had a husband with three vices, all starting with an A: alcoholic, abuser, adulterer. Years of his betrayals had ground down Lima and Faiza but the final blow came when her husband decided to leave them for another woman.

Soon Lima's visits were no longer relegated to the living room. She usually ate lunch with us, then spent the afternoons quietly lying on my bed, reading magazines. No one bothered her. Faiza was as quiet and immobile as her mother. She sat staring blankly at the toys I shared with her. I sensed a torrent of questions behind her blankness. She knew I didn't have answers and I was certain she would never ask. But I was anxious to know the reason behind Lima's long and languorous afternoons on my bed.

In three months' time, when Lima's stomach grew large and tight like a watermelon, I was even more confused. By now, she was a permanent part of my bed, a gargantuan specimen hidden under a pile of nonsense magazines, while an entire household of people she hardly knew went about their business. After a few more months, when I could no longer bear to have my bed dominated by a bloated stranger lying belly up and mute, I decided to withhold my dolls from Faiza. Childishly vengeful, I hoped my rudeness would make them leave. My reprisal had no effect on Faiza, who remained as stoic as ever. Her life had taught her exactly what she needed to know in order to survive. She sat alone on the floor, resignedly doodling on a piece of notebook paper. Not once did she look up at me and, if our eyes met by accident, I could read nothing in her vacant stare.

Frustrated beyond words, I went to my mother and demanded an explanation for the intrusion.

'Because she is our guest,' replied my mother, cautiously.

'But other guests don't come every day to sleep on my bed.'

'Well, Lima is pregnant so it's hard for her to move.' Mother paused and sighed. 'Listen to me,' she said, 'Lima is going to have a baby but she's very worried because she doesn't know where the baby's father is.'

'Why not?'

'You're too young to understand.'

'Tell me, please, I can keep a secret,' I insisted.

'It's not a secret, sweetheart. It's just very complicated.'

'Are you helping her find the baby's father?'

'Yes, I'm helping her. Please try to understand, my love.'

I didn't understand much about the baby's father's disappearance or how my mother could help. But I understood the crushed look on Lima's face as she lay helpless on my narrow bed, recognised the humiliated contours of Faiza's neck and shoulders when I snatched my dolls away and left her to play alone. They were both signs of shame, the same kind of shame I had felt before the pir, or standing on the red bench under the sun. Suddenly I knew exactly how Lima and Faiza felt – though I didn't fully fathom the reasons behind those feelings. Suddenly I could see the tension roiling beneath the unmoving planes of their faces, could see right through to their ebbing spirits, trying hard to stay ashore. I started sharing my dolls with Faiza again, though she had noticeably less interest in them now, as if she knew that dolls merely replicated the futile structure of human relationships. Some afternoons, as we played on the floor, Faiza and I could hear Lima sobbing softly, though we both pretended not to hear.

Lima extricated herself from our lives as suddenly as she had appeared. Even Uncle Karim didn't know exactly what happened to her. He had heard different rumours through friends about Lima giving birth to a boy and moving to a different city, while others thought her husband might have returned to her.

I can still visualise her defenceless form on my bed; I can still feel the weight of her deprecation. And I can taste her shame as I nurse my own.

One summer Amol hung a nylon rope swing from the rungs in the partial ceiling of our veranda. Naveen and I swayed for hours and stared out at the sprawling soccer field across from our house. Sometimes I noticed a young man standing at the edge of the field, staring in the direction of our house. When I told Naveen, she smiled shyly and told me not to look at him. Around that time, Moinul came to live with us.

Moinul, a distant relative from my grandmother's town, was disturbingly tall, but more disturbing was the rumour we'd heard about him from our mother. Moinul, who openly claimed to hate his entire family, had threatened to kill his youngest sister by slitting her veins in her sleep. Naturally, we were afraid of him, but my mother reassured us that Moinul was trying to find work in Dhaka and would only stay with us for a short while. At first he seemed harmless. When he wasn't out looking for 'work' (though what kind of work he was suited for, none of us knew), he sat on the steps outside, smoked and munched on betel leaves. If he saw any of us nearby, he'd pull out some ancient-looking candy from his shirt pocket and offer them to us. One day he grabbed my shoulders and squeezed my cheeks hard. He told me that I was growing as plump as a football and that soon he would have to carry my ovoid form to the soccer field for a few kicks. My feelings towards him solidified into resentment.

One afternoon Moinul came home early. I was on the swing and Naveen leaned over the balustrade, staring out at the soccer field. Mother must have come up behind Naveen and noticed the chap she was gazing at. I didn't know it, but my parents had already discovered the suggestive exchange of looks and smiles between Naveen and the soccer-field chap. When questioned in private, Naveen had revealed that the boy had sent her some sort of love note which, of course, she had not kept. My father was furious enough to pick up a slipper and whack Naveen's twelve-year-old face. He threatened to discipline her much more severely if she continued the misconduct.

So when Mother caught Naveen making eyes with the same boy again, her maternal heart grew apprehensive with dark thoughts. Why was Naveen being so reckless? What if the chap was a street hooligan? There were stories in the newspapers of young girls being abducted, raped, or defaced with acid.

In a moment of well-meaning weakness – but weakness nevertheless – my mother went to Moinul, who was smoking on the steps, and sought his help. 'Moinul, would you tell that boy not to stare at my house or send my daughter notes? Don't be too rude to him, you understand? Just tell him to scoot from here – firmly but nicely,' she asked.

Moinul quietly finished his cigarette, taking time to snuff it beneath one, boot-clad foot, caked with mud. Then he sauntered out to the soccer field. From a distance, it seemed like a polite chat ensued between Moinul and the young chap. To our surprise, the fellow followed Moinul back to our house.

'Auntie,' Moinul addressed my mother, 'I just wanted to know a little more about our friend here and thought it might be better to chat inside than in the middle of the street.'

'Oh I see.' Mother was looking uncomfortable. Naveen had disappeared.

'Auntie, let me take him to my room to ask him a few questions. Don't worry, it won't take long.'

'Moinul, wait. Why don't we all talk here?' my mother suggested.

'Auntie, I told you I'd take care of this. It'll just be a man-to-man chat. You relax,' he smiled sweetly.

Feeling increasingly puzzled, I went to look for Naveen and found her lying face down on her bed, her arms wound tightly around her pillow.

The next thing we heard were loud, dull thuds as though heavy sacks of rice were being unloaded on a hard cement floor. We heard the beginnings of screams, hastily muffled. My mother, Amol, Naveen and I rushed to Moinul's room but found the door locked. In between our frantic banging and screaming, we could hear a tedious thump thump thumping followed by the thwacking of Moinul's big black boots. Occasionally, Moinul would cry, 'I'll kill you, sisterfucker. That'll teach you to write love notes.'

Moinul opened the door only when my mother threatened to call the police. He charged about the room, snorting like a bull. He was a hungry carnivore, interrupted just before the kill. Given the opportunity, he might have cut anyone's throat right then.

'Moinul,' screeched Mother, 'where is he? Where is the boy?'

Before Moinul had a chance to answer, my mother pushed me back towards the door. I wasn't allowed to see the gory scene inside Moinul's room, and I couldn't bring myself to ask Naveen if she had seen it either. I will never know who carried the limp and bleeding body out of the house, but I will always remember the thin, bright trail of blood left behind. I also recall a long, rasping sound, like someone trying hard to breathe through a crushed ribcage. As they carried him away, the rasping blended into the susurration of a quiet, breezy evening.

Moinul left us the next day. He disappeared into the morning haze and we never saw him again. My father mumbled something about the inconvenience of putting up a house-guest for too long. But even after Moinul was gone, his venom remained with us for a long time. We stopped talking about the events of that dreadful afternoon but we could not forget about it. Every time our eyes fell on an empty spot in the vast soccer field, we deftly averted our gazes.

While none of us felt singularly responsible for what had happened, what we did feel was a kind of collective shame – shame for witnessing a wrong, for not being able to prevent it, for trusting someone's life with Moinul, for being human. In the wake of what we had experienced, we'd all been diminished in different ways, yet none of us dared to say it lest we broke the fragile peace that hung over our household. After that fateful day, if my mother caught Naveen or me leaning over the balustrade and staring down at the street, she'd pause for a second and then quietly turn around. Naveen seemed quieter too but in a hardened kind of way. The taut lines on her face were defence lines that no one dared to cross.

I wasn't really sure what I felt except a gnawing sense of discomfort that I couldn't shake off.

It was the nature of shame: it never left me because I never allowed it to. I held on to my shame, tightly, desperately, afraid that if I revealed it, I would fall further into its abysmal pit. Shame urged me to grow inwards, to become invisible. And I learned that if I stopped noticing myself, others did the same. If I didn't feel my body any more, then it stopped taking up any space. If I stopped listening to my feelings then I could no longer hear the toll of shame. People saw me as shy, quiet, introverted. But I wasn't as shy as I was invisible. Not as quiet as I was keen on not being heard. Words gurgled up to my lips but I pushed them back down, refusing to give them shape or form. For I chose to remain invisible.

The Naked Ghosts were discovered by Shonali, our one-eyed ayah. Shonali, who had been with us since I was a baby, wore her blind, bulging blue eye as a mark of her supernatural wisdom. With her blind eye she claimed to see things that a normal eye could not. There was one corner of our roof where a mango tree leaned forward to create a cool green shade. There Shonali squatted every evening, sucking on a bidi, betel juice dripping from her mouth, while ghosts galore visited her. Some of them were torsoless, mere heads floating about aimlessly and some had Himalayan forms reaching the skies, their eyes as big as headlights. Despite the terror they provoked in us, we loved listening to Shonali's descriptions of those visiting spirits.

One evening she detected, through the dense foliage of mango leaves, a pair of nangta bideshi bhooths – the naked ghosts of a white sahib and memsahib. This piqued our interest immediately. Naveen and I joined Shonali in the shade of the mango tree every day after dark in the hope of seeing two naked white ghost-bodies. Shonali was aghast to find that they did not return, not even for the benefit of her prophetic blind eye. 'I saw them I tell you,' she protested, 'the memsahib had breasts like long thin mangoes and the sahib, oh my God – sweeties, promise you won't tell your mother – the sahib was hung like a bull!'

Naveen expressed her disgust, 'Watch your mouth Shonali, what kind of talk is this!'

I secretly wanted Shonali to continue. What else had she seen? Did ghosts copulate?

A few weeks later, when the foreign ghosts still failed to appear, we lost interest and left Shonali alone. But she hadn't lied to us after all. Months after she had first located the bideshi bhooth couple, she came running to our room and urged us to follow her to the roof. That night, we finally saw the mythical Naked Ghosts.

Naveen and I strained to see through the gaps in the leafy darkness. A young white woman with short blond hair, completely naked, leaned over what seemed like a table and appeared to be chopping something. A man came up from behind her, also completely naked, and handed her something which she added to her preparations. What Shonali had not perceived with her one-eyed vision was the shape of a window, framing the young couple cooking in the nude. What Shonali had seen, correctly, was the sahib's bull-like endowment. 'Do you see it?' she cackled demonically, unperturbed by the fact that her ghosts had turned into humans. 'Do you see how his manhood sways and swaggers?'

'No,' I said, equally animated, 'Where? Where? Show me!'

But Naveen was already pulling me away from the sight of the Naked Ghosts. 'They're not ghosts, you idiot,' she wailed, 'they're human beings. And we should be ashamed of ourselves for staring at them.'

When Shonali wasn't smoking bidis or ghost-hunting, she turned her attention to Amol the cook. She cracked jokes to make him laugh and made up all sorts of affectionate pet names for him. She sat on her haunches while he worked, telling him long, painful stories of her childhood in the hope of gaining his sympathy. Amol routinely rejected her warmth, engaging her in fights more readily than conversation. We were used to their daily scuffles but one day I chanced upon an unusual scene.

I strolled into the kitchen to find Amol sitting on a wooden stool clutching an untouched plate of rice on his lap. His eyes protruded out of their sockets, the veins on his temples throbbed. Not four feet away from him, stood Shonali, hands on her hips, her face an unfathomable mingle of outrage and amusement. She was screaming obscenities at him and there was an undertone of anger in her voice. It sounded as if Shonali's words, though coated with rage, were driven by a more poignant urgency. Amol, of course, didn't understand the cause of her ire, as was clear from his expression. His breath came in short, heavy puffs as he cursed at her. For a time, neither of them acknowledged my presence and it took considerable work to find out what had passed. 'She farted on my food!' spat out Amol. 'As soon as I sat down to eat, she hitched up her sari, revealed her hideous bottom and farted on my food!' He shuddered.

I turned to Shonali, fully expecting her to defend herself against such an implausible accusation. To my disconcertion, Shonali began to giggle, then chortled and finally let loose great guffaws, doubling over. Betel juice and spit dribbled down her chin as she threw her head back, flashing her black teeth and tongue. Her laughter soon turned into spasms of cough that suggested a deep, glutinous congestion. And the tremendous effort of laughing and coughing at the same time produced an outpouring of farts, a long, successive line of small explosive bursts that smelled like rotten eggs. The farting brought forth further entertainment for her, initiating the laughing-coughing-farting cycle all over again.

Amol seemed to teeter between horror and resignation. He settled on horror, flung his plate aside and fled from the kitchen. I waited until Shonali's convulsions came to an end. She wiped her mouth with the edge of her sari. An uncharacteristic calm settled upon her features as she slowly prepared a plate of food for herself. With great satisfaction, she climbed on to the deserted stool and started to eat. It occurred to me that Shonali had bared her bottom to Amol to justify being rejected by him. Her retaliation was an act of validation. She wanted Amol to bow down to her ugliness if not her appeal. Unlike me, she had no shame; she refused to be invisible.

*   *   *

On the first floor of our building, there was Bablu, the Imitator of Frogs. So well could he imitate a frog that the first time I heard him, I thought we were being invaded by frogs. From my window, I watched his spiky head bent over a cement water tank where plastic cars and boats floated amidst small fish and turtles. He spoke to the fish and turtles in his frog voice and occasionally, when he sensed my presence, he glanced up to nod at me. Sometimes, when I saw Bablu sweating in the roiling heat, speaking the language of frogs, I envied the way he seemed so sure of his occupation. I longed to learn the language of frogs but at twelve, I was too shy and tongue-tied around boys to approach Bablu.

Then came the week of praying for rain. Heat rose from the earth in dry vapours but the raindrops clung like festering pustules inside the greyish clouds. Bablu stood by his water tank and looked at his dejected turtles, motionless from the heat. He scratched his head and looked up, asking suddenly 'Hey, do you want to come down here?' For the first time, I heard his normal voice. How unsure it sounded without the hoarse frog-like baritones.

'Why don't you meet me at the ledge on the roof?' I said.

I had recently learned from an informative teen romance series that if a boy were to propose something, the proposal must be accepted on slightly different terms. Bablu didn't seem to mind. He found me lying flat on my back on the precarious ledge of tin and cement, strictly prohibited to all the young-sters in the building because of its unstable constitution. We huddled in my little corner where I'd lined up a few old gift boxes, some paper and pencil, a flask of orange juice. I offered Bablu orange juice. 'No, thanks. Do you want to smoke? I have a cigarette,' he said. I had never smoked a real cigarette. Silently I received my first cigarette from him, a wrinkled, slightly damp Star 555, the same kind my father smoked.

The first inhalation made me gaze up and down with light-headed amazement. The rain clouds moved above us, blocking the orange sun and casting a purplish hue across the thirsty grey sky. Down below, the street was an uprising of sound and sight. A vendor selling spicy rice puffs rolled his cart along, shrieking out the names of his goodies to potential customers. A procession of female factory workers made their way home in a noisy cluster of colourful saris and ribbons. Rickshawallahs zoomed by with their empty vehicles. Was the street always this active? Why hadn't I noticed before? Euphoria flooded me as the tobacco hit my head, followed by a bout of coughing. Bablu patted me on the back. I had forgotten he was there.

'I've never smoked before,' I apologised.

'It's all right, don't be embarrassed. Um ... may I share something else with you?'

'Of course.'

From the folds of his shirt, he pulled out a tattered-looking pamphlet.

'What is it?'

'It's a book ... with pictures. Take a look,' he replied nervously.

He handed me a yellowish, moth-eaten newsprint copy of a pornographic magazine. On the faded cover was the picture of a naked woman, bent from the waist, her huge bare bottom revealed to the beholder. If you looked closely, you could see that she peered back up at you through the inverted V of her legs, wearing a look of utter despair on her face. Bablu had made a tiny circle on the woman's exposed privates with a red marker. He pointed at the circle and gushed, 'Is that it? Is that where it goes in?'

I could not turn the pages any further. Bablu did the job for me. One by one, he showed me the pictures in the newsprint leaflet, displaying the animal business of naked bodies, and I, looking on in the purplish light at those strange men and women, wondered whether there was pleasure or pain in those peculiar-looking, almost grotesque acrobatics. I could see Bablu's eyes gleaming. Part of me was intrigued by his audacity, part of me was repulsed by it. Part of me wanted to look through every picture again and part of me wanted to tear the book to shreds. Part of me wanted to rip my dress and show him where that red-circled spot existed in a real girl and part of me wanted to push him off the ledge.

Bablu put his hand over mine and moved closer. I smelled his breath. Did he really smell like frogs? A big, fat drop of rain fell on one of the lascivious pages. Seizing the opportunity, I looked up at the sky and yelled, 'Look, it's about to rain!' Bablu jumped, the moment was broken. He dropped my hand, snatched his precious pages, climbed off the ledge and disappeared.

It rained that afternoon and the inflamed earth cooled its sore and tired body. From the next day onwards, Bablu the Imitator of Frogs was back at his tank but we never renewed our brief alliance. Every time I passed by him I cringed at the vision of a despondent face, staring up at me through an upside-down V.

*   *   *

The same year I parted ways with Bablu the Imitator of Frogs, Mala came to work in our house. Tiny Mala, the first adolescent girl who worked for us, had a big-hearted understanding of the universe. She did not begrudge it anything. She prattled continually and laughed even more. For reasons unknown, the mere act of carrying heavy bucketfuls of water sent her into peals of laughter. If a man leered at her on the street, she spat at him and scampered away, giggling. When we returned from school she would be squatting under the midday sun, washing clothes in the little cement basin on the roof and the sight of us would make her bob up and down with joy, sending soap suds and frothy water flying above her sprightly head. She accepted my old discarded clothes as if they were priceless pieces from fashion collections.

Not even the barriers of language held Mala's vivacious spirit in check. She watched English television shows with us, grunting and nodding at all the right cues. After watching *The A-Team*, she ran her fingers through her thick hair and expressed, rather seriously, the wish to get a Mohawk like Mr T. Her admiration of him was partly due to her conclusion, that Mr T, with his excessive collection of gold chains, was the richest man in the world.

Mala came to me one day and made an earnest request. 'Will you teach me how to read and write?' she asked.

'Do you want to go to school?' I responded, a bit perplexed, as no other maid in our home had ever made such a request.

'No, I just want to read books.'

'What kind of books do you want to read?'

'Historical ones,' she said, 'about kings and queens.'

I agreed to teach Mala. I had noticed her in the mornings

when we wolfed down our breakfast before school. Mala hovered in the background with a mop, her eyes lingering on our schoolbags, trailing our steps as we dashed to catch the schoolbus. I knew how much she would have loved to climb into that bus with us, just to see if everything she imagined about the world of books and kings and queens were true.

The lessons began and my student had more to say than I had bargained for. Why do people speak in different languages? Why don't animals speak? What language will we speak after death? I assumed a contemplative persona in the hope of fooling her about the extent of my own knowledge.

'Read,' I told her with great solemnity, 'and the answers will come to you.'

I could not have known that the pretence of such solemnity would break down one quiet afternoon, when Mala appeared a half hour early for her lesson and discovered me poring over a lingerie catalogue I'd stolen from my mother's dresser. Without hesitation or permission, she yanked it from me and held to her face the picture of a buxom blonde, breasts spilling out of a sheer pink bra. I tried to snatch the magazine from her but Mala moved away just in time.

'Wait,' she said with unusual sobriety, 'why are you looking at this?'

Why *was* I looking? How could I tell her about my meeting with Bablu, the thrill and the horror of it? How could I tell her that to erase the disturbing images of those ravaged bodies in the magazine, I searched for bodies more temperate and tender, swelling with the possibility of something more mystifying? How could I explain to her that which was not entirely clear to me?

Mala, however, had more clarity than I, on the subject of bodies. 'I have seen many naked bodies,' she said. 'They didn't look anything like this.' Haltingly, she described to me a little village, a one-room shack and five bodies in it – herself, her parents, her brother and his wife. At the end of the day, everyone in their tiny cabin laid down their straw mats wherever they chose on the mud floor and slept next to each other in the unpartitioned room. In the darkness, made partly visible by moonlight streaming in through the thatched roof, Mala had watched the shadowy figures of men and women engaged in acts of love. She had seen her brother rip off his wife's sari as she writhed underneath him, their bare chests heaving. She had watched her own father make love to her mother. In the morning, everything was normal when the sun rose in the eastern sky. Everybody casually rolled up their mats, drank tea in a cosy circle and went about their day. New babies were born into these cramped habitats and they too grew up with the same uncensored view of love.

I was mesmerised by her stories, and then, as if moved by a magnetic force, I was drawn to her face, her milky brown skin, the concave space below her neck. Or was it she who looked at me like that?

I had never touched anyone in an intimate way. Instead of the man's face I had always imagined in my fantasies of intimacy, here was a young girl my own age, with wise eyes and a wicked smile. My own body was betraying me. A touch, a caress, was all I wanted. My hands reached forward with dizzy longing. I felt the warm cotton softness of her skin. A silky sensation spread through me. I felt no shame, only pleasure at the unfamiliar touch. I wanted nothing more than the moment to last. That was precisely when Naveen walked in. Both Mala and I recoiled with sharp intakes of breath, a lowering of our eyes. The wanton blush spreading across my cheeks was mirrored in Mala's.

What would I say to Mala if I saw her now? Would I ask her if she lived in a one-room shack with many others? Would we be so bold as to discuss that extraordinary moment we had shared? Or would we politely greet each other then turn the other way? I do not know. But I know that seeing Mala again may disturb the delicate stance of the memory I wish to keep intact, the memory of my first erotic touch, its incipient joy quelled as quickly as it had bloomed.

Gowsia Market was the most sensory of Dhaka experiences. I loved it and I abhorred it. My mother shopped there for uncommon paraphernalia and she loved to take one of her children along as company. There was nothing we couldn't find in Gowsia Market, which teemed with hosts of hawkers selling everything from bobby pins and buttons to hundreds of varieties of dress materials, laces, saris, multi-coloured glass bangles, earrings, necklaces, precious jewellery of gold, silver and diamonds, toiletries, cosmetics, perfumes, shoes, home decor, curtains, flowers, dinnerware, pots and pans.

Some stalls were mere squares, held up by four sturdy poles, covered above and on three sides by a patch of tarpaulin, under which unsteady cardboard shelves displayed miscellaneous items. The bigger shops had clear glass cabinets with neon lights casting a harsh glow on the displayed goods. Adolescent hawkers carrying large wooden trays hung around their necks with dirty cotton slings followed customers like pesky flies. They sold things like safety pins, cotton balls, mothballs and handkerchiefs.

Crowds gathered each day at Gowsia like a swarm of bees around a honeycomb. They pushed their way through vigorously to avoid being brutally elbowed, shoved or trampled.

One section of the market was lined with food stalls choking the air with the zest of smoked meats, fried dough and burnt oil. The wooden benches in front of each stall were always bursting with people taking a break from shopping to gorge on chotpoti, bhelpuri, phuchka, fried chicken, French fries and kebab rolls. One of the best parts of our Gowsia trips was when my mother and I took a snack break. She would lead us to the Phuchka House and order two flaming hot plates of phuchka with extra chilli and tamarind sauce and steaming cups of oversweetened, overmilky coffee. Each burning bite of the chilli-stuffed phuchka was followed by a deliciously painful sip of scalding coffee.

But something happened one day to break the familiar tempo of our Gowsia trip. My mother and I had just finished our phuchka and plunged back into the hive of people, moving shoulder to shoulder. She moved expertly forward, pulling me by one hand, while I tried to keep up with her. We were tightly wedged inside the heart of the crowd when I felt a sweaty, hot palm slither up my childish frock and grip my bottom. I was astonished. Had a small animal crept up my thighs? Was someone groping for a lost partner's hand and mistakenly come to settle upon my bottom?

Although I still held my mother's hand, her face was not visible to me. A lady in a blue cloak had lodged herself between my mother and me and all I could see were the backs or sides of people bunched together like sheaves of coriander. Taking a deep breath, I used my free hand to reach behind and grab the misbehaving hand but just then it pinched my bottom hard. The stinging pain made me turn around sharply in an attempt to find my offender. I barely managed to catch sight of a middle-aged man with a large moustache, standing directly behind me, holding a child in one arm, while using his other to fondle me.

He was sucking his teeth, face tensed with concentration. As soon as he caught me looking, his expression gave way to a stunned discomfort and he hastily released my bottom. There was not enough space for him to move away so he stared stonily ahead, pretending to be just another body in the slow-moving swarm. Being only nine years old, I struggled for an appropriate retaliation. As my mother pulled me away, all I could do was look back at that abominable man and whisper, 'Shame-shame.'

Somewhere in my soul is a little girl, still waiting for forgiveness, be it God's or my father's or mother's; somewhere in me is a feeling of guilt, of shame, so ingrained, I can almost touch it. When I peer into my childhood, I never see a child. And even if I do, I never feel the child's innocence or exuberance. Rather, I see a child who is trying hard to grow up before her time. I see a child who senses that curiosity is sinful and defiance is unpardonable.

I remember myself at nine, in the dark under the blanket. I am running my fingers up my thighs, hesitantly finding and stroking a spot, pushing and probing further. Warmth and wetness; tingling and tension. My small body grows taut. I increase the friction between my skin and finger and reel from pleasure. Then the darkness is invaded. My mother lifts the blanket and lets out a horrified yelp.

'What do you think you're doing?' she growls.

I blink at her, confused. Have I done something bad? She never says. Never has to. I already know from the disgust spreading across her beautiful features, from the sharp sting of her palm across my cheek, the pearl and gold ring on her index finger scraping the bridge of my nose.

Birth is as much a disembodiment as it is a compilation, a conformation. As the umbilical cord is cleaved, once and for all, the separation and disconnection that make each newborn wail in anxiety seem unpreventable. Nature, in its complexity and effectiveness, prepares us for what is ahead. As we slide down the dark passage of our first shelter, helpless against the expunging currents of a suddenly rough sea, we may apprehend that we are merely passing through the eye of the storm. We emerge on the other side, no longer attached to another being and step into the world as one body, one mind. It is a consciousness that is unique to ourselves and that we will define now on our own. And the beginning of consciousness was, for me, the awareness of everything that was wrong.

One of Nanu's special recipes consisted of a mouth-watering concoction of fried red chillies, onions and coriander leaves. She called it pora morich bhorta – it felt like a ball of fire in my mouth, especially with steaming hot rice, but I loved it. I waited for Nanu to visit so she could make this spicy delight for me. During one such visit, I came home from school to find that lunch was being served but there was no sign of Nanu's morich bhorta. I threw my backpack on the floor and ran to find Nanu. She was busy talking to Mother. She swatted away my queries distractedly and when I persisted for her attention, it was my mother who answered me.

'Stop this nagging,' she ordered. 'It's too late to make morich bhorta now. Wash your hands and come to the table.'

I turned to Nanu, desperately pleading. I knew she could make the bhorta in less than fifteen minutes if she wanted to. I had seen her do it a thousand times. I knew the steps by heart: briefly heat the chillies in a low fire before frying them in mustard oil, chop the onions and coriander and mix them all together . . . I couldn't think any more. I licked my lips, still sure that Nanu would save the day. I waited for her to tell Mother that it was all right, that she would make the bhorta. But Nanu seemed unsure, uncomfortable. Her silence filled the room.

'I said wash your hands and come to the table,' bellowed Mother.

'No!' I screamed, with all my ten years of might. 'I will not wash and I don't want to eat!'

Nanu cringed and finally opened her mouth to say something but Mother was already pulling me towards the bedroom. I, kicking and screaming, tried to wrench free from her painful grip, bumping against walls and furniture as she yanked me forward relentlessly. She released her iron grip only when she pushed me into the room. 'Stay here and go hungry if you like. That'll teach you.'

I crawled under the covers and cried, feeling angrier at not being able to fight the overwhelming tears. Even as I wept, a part of me kept waiting for someone to come and find me and lead me back to the dining table where I could hear everyone sitting down for the meal. I could hear their conversation and the tinkling of silverware. The familiar scents of daal and curry and rice made me almost faint with hunger. Had everyone forgotten me?

In truth, no one had forgotten. And it wasn't that no one cared about me either. Everyone kept their distance, because I was undergoing the all-too-important ritual of righting the wrong. I was being punished. Punishment, whether big or small, was my biggest constant in an otherwise unpredictable world. I was all too familiar with it. I had to pay my penance for desiring the wrong thing at the wrong time and then lashing out, when denied. I ought to be ashamed and I was. What I didn't understand was why it was so wrong of me to ask for what seemed like such a simple thing. The world was becoming an increasingly complex place, where even the smallest pleasure came at an enormous price. That night, Nanu made her famous morich bhorta. She made a big bowl of it and smiled at me encouragingly. For some reason, I cannot recall whether I ate any of it. But I remember that my appetite for anything spicy changed from that day onwards. It was as if my tastebuds held their ground in quiet protest while I slowly conformed into an obedient child. Or perhaps it was my body's way of punishing itself for lusting so shamelessly after such a banal pleasure. Either way, I have not been able to savour or stomach anything hot and spicy since that day, least of all, that delectable morich bhorta of my childhood.

Years later, in college, my friend Anna asked me why I was always so punitive towards myself. 'Why do you always sell yourself short?' she asked, accusingly. 'You're always second guessing yourself and you cower in silence even when you know you're right. You're so damn apologetic!'

I had never thought of myself like that. I came from a world where apologies were a way of life. The most special ones were reserved for God, then your elders, then your teachers, then those peers who were better than you at something or another (and there was always someone better at something). You apologised because you weren't good enough and, if you were, you had to aspire to be something even bigger and better. The gratification was not so much in being something as it was in trying to be something else. But now I was in another universe. Perhaps, this was my chance. 'I'm sorry,' I said, 'I hadn't realised—'

'Stop!' Anna held up a hand, a smile breaking across her lips. 'Start over. This time without an apology.'

I had to smile.

'Consider yourself great at everything, Maria,' Anna said. 'You should wake up every morning and give yourself at least one compliment before you start your day.'

'C'mon, Anna.'

'Why not? My mom told me to do this when I was going through a hard time in high school.'

I stared at Anna. I wanted to ask her if she had ever prayed for forgiveness without even knowing why she needed to be forgiven. Had she ever apologised to her father or mother for not being exactly the way they had imagined she would be? I wanted to ask her if doubt and guilt clouded her every thought so that silence was often a better recourse than words. But I knew that asking her these things would simply give her a skewed view of the other world where I grew up. The world I still loved and was trying to escape from. The world that was now a shadow – faceless, blurry, yet always with me. A world that came to me in contrasting shades of mortification and solace. A world that was seldom exonerating but hardly indifferent and never ordinary. I cared for it in the same way it had cared for me – with utmost devotion and an utter lack of understanding.

Beloved Strangers

The room is square and semi-dark; heavy curtains block the sunlight. There are two single beds joined together to make one large double bed where I sleep with my sisters. Two wooden dressers, one black, one brown, stand on either side of the bed. Through the crack in the door I can see the leg of my new Barbie on top of the brown dresser. I also see my mother sitting on the bed with her harmonium, flipping through sheets of music. Her guru sits across from her, cross-legged, humming and tapping his fingers on the polished surface of the instrument. I want my doll but I dare not step inside the room. When my mother practises her music the world is her enemy.

Until she was six years old, my mother lived in the tiny, sleepy town of Comilla, about a hundred kilometres south-east of Dhaka. Then her father died unexpectedly from kidney failure at the age of forty, and his passing left my grandmother a widow at twenty-four. My grandmother moved into her brother's family with three small children of whom Mother was the second. From then on, they moved from one town to another due to the nature of Mother's maternal uncle's work.

Mother spoke of her uncle with a rare fondness. He had loved her like a father, pampered her more than his own children and made sure that, despite the frequent relocations, Mother was not deprived of what pleased her most: music. Wherever they went, he found a music teacher for her, and by the time she was a teenager, she had won a number of trophies and certificates for her musical talent at school and other local functions. At the end of high school, when most of her friends left their small town to go to college in the big city, my mother didn't care. She was absorbed in her music, ecstatic that the local radio stations had started to schedule her for regular appearances.

The first time it was 'arranged' for my father to see my mother as a prospective bride was during one of her weekly radio programmes. The two families thought it best that my father should see her from afar, without her knowledge. Meeting face to face, even if chaperoned, was not considered proper. So my father turned up at the radio station, stood outside a glass-enclosed studio and watched a skinny nineteen-year-old singing in a voice so mesmerising that he forgot why he was there.

My father went home to tell everyone he had found his bride. My mother went home, completely unaware that her song had led her to her future husband. Though Mother knew she would have to consider marriage sooner or later, given her mother's exhaustive search for a groom, it did not stop her from feeling a jolt of panic when my father, eager and smitten, asked for her hand. She was hesitant to leave the uncomplicated rhythm of her life where music was her only partner, but how much longer could she continue to refuse her suitors? Had she chosen to refuse, however, deciding to pursue music instead of marriage, her uncle and grandmother promised to stand by her. But Mother agreed to the match with an unexpected ferocity. 'I'm ready,' she declared, 'start the preparations right away.' I presume she wanted to put an end to the constant reminder that she was her widowed mother's last burden.

Once she gave her consent, my mother refused to discuss the matter any further, letting her family busy themselves with the minutiae of the wedding. Finding her in bed in the middle of the day, while the house bustled with wedding activity, her grandmother approached her quietly.

'Are you well, dear?' she asked Mother.

'Yes I am.'

'Don't you at least want to know what he looks like?'

'What's the point? I'm still going to marry him,' said Mother.

'You don't have to marry him if you don't want to.'

'It doesn't matter now.'

'Don't say that!'

'Fine, tell me what he looks like,' my mother said in a resigned voice.

Her grandmother brightened. 'Oh he's very handsome, more fair-skinned than any man I've seen. His skin is so light you can see the veins underneath. Such white-white children you'll have!'

The faintest smile flitted across my mother's face. Her grandmother sighed and placed a gentle hand on her grand-daughter's head.

The wedding took place in Comilla, and on the night of the wedding, Ismail the servant boy fell into a cauldron of boiling milk and went half insane. Later he confided that the djinns had come to him when everyone was busy with the festivities. They came in the guise of three exquisite and identical young women. In the smoky kitchen, a horrified Ismail recognised their unblinking stares and backed away from them until he fell into the drum of scalding milk. He never heard the message they had come to deliver. The sounds of firecrackers and wedding music drowned his screams for help.

That same night, my father was to take his new bride and make the three-hour journey back to his Dhaka home. He had instructed his best friend to convert his small bachelor pad into a bridal suite, replete with flowers, candles and a heavy lace bedspread. A table was laden with trays of multi-coloured sweets and tall pitchers of almond and coconut milk. His friend waited to receive the exhausted bride and groom. But once the bride and groom were on their way, the driver turned around and announced that he was taking them to my father's sister's house.

'Why?' asked my bewildered father.

'It is your sister's order,' the driver shrugged.

My father opened his mouth to say something then closed it again. His older sister was not someone he could easily disobey. They reached her house well after midnight. Lifting the pleats of her heavy red sari off her dainty feet, my mother wearily made her way up the dark, cramped staircase. The maid sleepily warmed up some leftover fish curry from the night before. After dinner, my parents spent their wedding night in a tiny, airless room that had been hurriedly cleared for them, while, in another part of the city, a fragrant room with a dreamy white bed glowed softly until all the candles burned out.

In 1971, a year after their wedding, my parents lived in a bungalow on the top of a hill in Chittagong, where my father worked at the head office of the Bangladesh Tobacco Company. My mother stayed at home with one-year-old Naveen, an old Nepali ayah and Harun the cook. The garden was the best part of their sprawling colonial-style bungalow. Huge red dahlias and bushes of wild tulips sprung robustly out of the mountain earth. When the midday sun grew softer, the ayah took Naveen out in a stroller for long walks. My mother sat in the secluded garden and sipped cup after cup of tea. But the nights were bad. The sound of gunfire, sirens and hand grenades pierced the dark. Every once in a while, screams floated up the lonely mountain roads. Or did she imagine them? Once my mother woke up in the middle of the night and her heart caught in her throat at the sight of a malevolent face pressed against the windowpane. In the morning she found a bird, half-eaten and caked in dried blood, just outside her window and realised it had only been a fox. She must have been lonely, in that strange city, away from her family, in the middle of the war.

The officers came during the day, when my father was at work and Harun had gone to the market. The ayah was playing with Naveen. My mother opened the door. 'They were very tall,' she said. 'Tall in that Pakistani way.' Their eyes swept over her slim body. She was small, like most Bengali women. They were polite, even when they walked into our living room, uninvited. They didn't raise their voices or utter obscenities. They walked in as if they were always going to walk into our house, as if our house was not the sacred body that gave us shelter but a profane body that could be entered by anyone. My mother didn't try to stop them. She stood near the door and watched. Then they heard my sister's voice, chattering away with the ayah. A child? A girl? They must see her, immediately.

Things were shifting, happening too fast, as if in a disjointed dream. The ayah stifled a scream as one of the officers took Naveen from her arms. The next second, her jaw dropped as the officer hugged Naveen to his chest and kissed her on both cheeks. 'I have a daughter, just her age,' he said. The officers gave my sister a small piece of candy before they left.

The war ended in a year. East Pakistan gained its independence from West Pakistan and Bangladesh was born out of the dismemberment. Outside a beautiful bungalow on a hill, on quiet afternoons, sat the solitary figure of a young woman, her spirit moving above and beyond the mountains.

My mother is afraid of time.

Instead of eating her fruit, she has the unusual habit of rubbing their slimy insides on her face, neck and décolleté. Each morning at the breakfast table she amasses piles of fruit skin on the side of her plate while she rubs the sticky flesh on her skin. Bits of papaya, avocado and grapefruit jiggle on her upper lip as she schools us on the different minerals and vitamins present in each fruit. Papaya tightens the pores. Avocado replenishes the natural oils in skin, giving it a plump, youthful look. Grapefruit hydrates the epidermis, smoothing lines and wrinkles. It seems that each different property she mentions is important for the fulfilment of only one desire: remaining young.

'I want to be twenty-five again,' she says so frequently it's almost as if she believes she can make it happen by sheer force of will.

In her own way, she does make it happen. My mother refuses to reveal her age to anyone. She reddens with indignation if the rest of us reveal our real ages, giving people a clue as to how old our mother might be.

'You're not thirty,' she says to me firmly on my thirtieth birthday, 'You're twenty-eight.'

'I'm thirty, Mother.'

'You're twenty-eight,' she repeats, outraged.

So diligently has my mother played hide and seek with her age that I can no longer be sure, on any of her birthdays, how old she is going to be that year. For someone who finds time to be so precious, my mother wastes it lavishly. She is the most unpunctual person I know. Hours pass before she realises she has missed an appointment but the realisation leaves her unflustered. In her everlasting lateness, she presumes that time has not passed, that it is waiting for her.

'Why do you want to be twenty-five?' I ask Mother.

'Because it's the perfect age. You're neither young nor old, neither naive nor jaded. You have an idea of who you are but there's still so much left to discover,' she replies.

'But Mother, even if you were twenty-five again, everything would still happen all over again. Time wouldn't just stop.'

She gapes at me, silent and aghast, as if the thought has never crossed her mind.

At moments like this, it strikes me that what my mother wants, time and again, is not to replay or freeze her life, but to change its course. Like the times when we went to visit her best friend, Auntie Irene. Auntie Irene lived in a spacious, red-brick house by the lake with her husband and two sons. The furniture in their home was big, plush and shiny. There were Victorian-style silk curtains, Persian rugs and sturdy glass cabinets full of expensive-looking china. The drone of their air-conditioner never stopped and the entire house smelled like Cadbury chocolates. They were the only people we knew who had a real swimming pool in their backyard. Every time we crammed into our old white Toyota and pulled away after a day with Auntie Irene's family, Mother made it a point to sigh heavily, conspicuously. 'That's the kind of home I always thought I would have,' she'd remind us in her most plaintive tone. 'Beautiful, so spotless and stylish, like something out of a magazine.' Each of us, especially Father, was careful not to respond to her laments, because whoever did would immediately be held accountable for her unfulfilled dream. And yet, I had never seen my mother pick up a dust cloth or arrange a vase of flowers or fluff out the pillows on her perpetually unmade bed. Mother, in her characteristic wishfulness, expected the very earth to shift and shape into what her heart desired. And when it didn't, she'd go back and harshly rewrite her life a hundred times, sure that the real source of her sorrows lay in her past and not in her present. How many times had she said that if she had married later in life, or become famous like she was meant to, or had fewer children, or even if her father had been alive, everything else would have clicked right into place, like pieces of a puzzle. She walked into each room in our dishevelled home and imagined what it would be like if she could just replace the curtains, discard the furniture or change the colour of the walls. But never, not once, did she stand back to take a good look at what was already there, at what might already have been beautiful had she stopped to notice.

Sometime in the middle of second grade, I discovered a pair of scissors in Nanu's knitting basket and felt an overpowering urge to rip to shreds the curtains and sheets and upholstery that Mother so hated. I adopted a very particular style of destruction, always cutting a perfect little triangle into the fabric, lifting it up ever so gently and then smoothing it back into place so no one would notice. As soon as I destroyed something, I was horribly plagued by the need to repair the damage and reverse the imperfection I had created. What would it take to mend the tear as seamlessly as possible? I raided Nanu's basket for scraps of thread, which exactly matched the various fabrics I had vandalised and begged her to show me how to do a neat chain-stitch or a flawless hem. Nanu, an avid seamstress, was happy to teach me, pleased that I was showing signs of domesticity. It was hard not to get caught in my acts of treason but I managed to get away with it for a few weeks. Upon discovery, my weapon was confiscated and myself reprimanded although I thought I had been doing Mother a favour by giving her the opportunity to discard what she already disliked.

My quest for perfection was hardly over. The following year, I changed strategy. I found myself agonising over infinitesimal details of my room, my closet, my possessions. I never allowed anyone to touch my things. When I got my first Barbie doll, a long-haired blonde in a silver dress, I took her out of the pink paper box once a day to brush her hair and straighten her clothes, before putting her back inside. No matter how much Tilat cried, I would never place the glittering doll into her eager little hands. I got up extra early in the mornings to make my bed, clean out my desk and pack and re-pack my schoolbag. I tucked and re-tucked the bedsheets until my fingers became sore. I borrowed an old rag from the kitchen cupboard and each time I washed my hands or face I wiped both sink and counter clean of the last drop of water. I spent hours placing chairs and tables back at exactly the right angles and making sure all the shoes in the shoe rack were perfectly lined up. I organised my clothes until my palms were stiff from folding and refolding them. I never finished my schoolwork because I was too busy erasing every line I wrote. The inclination to perfect the imperfect began to affect my ability to concentrate on anything for long periods of time. Whereas before I spent only my idle time cleaning and refining, the obsession began to leak into my various other activities. As soon as I sat down with my textbooks, my eyes would start roaming and I'd run my fingers along the surface of my wooden desk for possible undulations. I would notice and feel distracted every time by the faint horizontal line on the wall where my books leaned against it and which I had washed a million times with soap and warm water. I would have to fight the stubborn urge to run for my cleaning rags for I knew that if I washed the wall any more the paint was likely to peel off. I collected different shades of brown magic markers with which I concealed the scrapes and chips on the old wooden desk, spots that only I could see. They swam before me like jagged obstacles in the path of my vision.

By the time I started high school, my handwriting improved dramatically although my notes grew sparse and full of gaps. In my green pencil box I carried a medley of sharpened pencils, ballpoint pens, four different erasers and a bottle of white correction fluid. In comparison to the other kids' workbooks, all of mine looked rickety thin, having torn out pages and pages due to crossed-out words or lines. One year, our class teacher convinced me to represent the school in a city-wide handwriting competition. It was my worst nightmare. I did not have the courage to say no to her, nor did I possess the nerves to survive the ordeal.

On the morning of the competition I arrived at Dhaka Art College where girls and boys sat cross-legged across the open courtyard, pieces of crisp white paper stuck to their writing boards. For the purpose of the contest, we had to copy a long newspaper article but we were allowed only one side of one piece of paper. Even before I began, visions of catastrophe froze me in my tracks: a leaking pen, sweat stains from my clammy palms, my white correction fluid overspilling and drying into uneven little ridges across the uniform surface of the paper . . . on and on my mind conjured torrid schemes of disaster. I watched the other contestants writing furiously, while I sat unable to start.

I may have earned more than an honourable mention if it hadn't been for the incomplete assignment I turned in. By the time I managed to overcome my fear of ravaging the white paper there were only fifteen minutes left of the thirty-five-minute contest. I wanted to forget the whole thing. What benefit was there to the artistry of handwriting when I could not boast mastery over the content of my books? But Mother, in a rare burst of pride, framed the certificate of honour and hung it on the wall. Would she have been proud if she knew the truth about my fears, my fixations? How many of her favourite things had I ruined only to mend them and alleviate my twisted need for neatness, the very quality that was now being celebrated within a framed certificate? How many times had I lied to her about losing my workbooks so that she would buy me new, clean ones? How many times had I deceived her into thinking that I was studying when I was simply rearranging my books yet again? And how would she feel if she caught me eyeing with secret disapproval the way she left stray hairs on her comb or cracked the brand-new spines of her books by leaving them open and face-down on the coffee table.

I wanted, very much, to end the Herculean task of tidying up the whole world but I was sickened, maddened, harassed by the need for balance, for equilibrium, for sparseness and symmetry. My mother, on the other hand, imagined the extreme, the impossible, anything to tip the scale from mundane to miraculous. In our own ways, we were both trying to achieve perfection. A perfection too crude, too literal.

If I am to paint a picture based on all the stories my mother discloses about her wedding and early years of marriage, it will be of a woman standing on a busy platform, alone, fervently waiting for her train to arrive. With passing years, the fervent look on her lovely face is tarnished by anger, panic, and finally, fatigue. For me, the question in this picture is not when the train will arrive but whether it will take her where she wants to go.

My mother said she wanted fame and stardom. 'Star' was the word she always used in reference to her music, not vocal artist, nor singer. At eight or nine years of age, I could somewhat grasp the glamour associated with fame. On the TV screen I saw famous stars walking up to sparkling podiums to receive gold and silver statues. From Mother, I heard stories about the popular music stars of our country performing all over the world, signing autographs for thousands of fans.

'The day someone asks for my autograph is the day I'll know I'm famous,' Mother used to say.

'Even if just one person asks you for it?' I asked.

'Yes, even if one person asks for it,' she replied.

Mother got her wish. But even though she signed a number of autographs for her fans, it never gratified her. The kind of fame she craved could not be gratified by ten, twenty or even a hundred applauding fans. The kind of fame she craved could never be gratified by several monthly performances on radio and television. She wanted her whole life to be centre stage, the spotlight on her, while she sang her heart out. She wanted trophies, foreign tours, newspaper articles, and an overbooked calendar to prove her worth and she wanted to be free to do all that.

I admired her ambition, the way it flashed across her features, the way it lifted her delicate chin. It was her despair that I had trouble with. Her despair, compelling her to banish everyone in her vicinity when she practised her music, as if she needed to guard her music, as if the very presence of another soul would derange her rhythm. The same despair made her clench her jaw when we crowded around her, vying for her attention as she tried to rest before a recording session.

When she despaired, so did I. Which is why, that afternoon, looking through the crack in the half-open door, I decided to send my mother a cryptic message. As soon as her practice ended, I crept up to her harmonium, found her music book and scribbled a note to her with my name signed underneath. 'You are my stepmother,' I wrote in my crooked handwriting. In my mind were the stepmothers of the fairy tales I'd read – unkind, unloving, neglectful.

A few days later, when she flipped through her notebook, my mother's face seemed to grow serious for a moment. I held my breath. If she were to ask me why I wrote what I wrote, I would tell her that I didn't really think she was unloving or unkind. I just wanted her to see me, behind my message, beyond my words. But she never asked.

Being kept away from my mother's music did not undermine my urge to sing; in fact, it had just the opposite effect. By the time I was nine years old, my favourite and secret pastime was to pretend play at being a singer. Once again, television fed my fantasies and I picked up enough moves to practise on my own. I flapped around in front of the bathroom mirror, using a pencil as a mike, my lips and eyelids slathered with my mother's maroon lipstick and glittery eye shadow. I played a wonderful audience to myself, clapping in rapt admiration at the end of each performance. Then I'd take a deep bow of appreciation. The joy of those moments was incomparable. When I sang, I felt free, my body inflated with possibility. Unlike my mother and her need to be alone with her music, I wanted to invite the whole world to share my joy with me when I sang. Of course I couldn't, because I knew Mother would not approve.

Outside my stuffy pink bathroom, reality became ineluctable. Mother and Father constantly argued about my mother's musical aspirations. It never occurred to me that my father was opposed to her music. Often, I caught him staring at her when she sang, a tender faraway look in his eyes, as if he was watching again his frail young bride-to-be with her enigmatic voice. Yet what brought forth his reticence when her music led her out of the house? How could he not see that she wanted to immerse herself in music as he immersed himself in his work? That she was as determined as he was to chart her territory and leave her mark?

Did he fear that if both of them were engrossed in their separate worlds the children would suffer? Or did he fear that the woman he loved so fiercely would be lost to him, if consumed by music? And he did love her fiercely. If he had his way, he would always have her around him. If my mother went out for a long time, my father grew increasingly restless. He hardly paid us any attention, staring hard at the television, though we knew his thoughts were elsewhere. He would jump at every sound or movement and, after a few hours had passed, would make repetitive queries on her whereabouts.

My mother, on the other hand, enjoyed her time alone. She hummed and pranced about the house. Often she dragged her harmonium from the music room to her bedroom, shut the door and spent hours singing or listening to music and reading. Her affection for my father was more subtle, reserved in special signs. Like the way she never called Father by his name, referring to him only as Jaanu, meaning heart. The far-too-obvious way in which she tried to suppress her excitement on the days he returned from a work tour abroad. The way she looked at their wedding photographs, sighed and said the same thing every time, 'Look how handsome your father was.'

Heaven forbid if mother had a radio programme or television shoot. Between her nervousness and my father's stubbornness, the conversations at meal times were poisonous.

'I may be gone for most of the day today,' my mother announced one morning. 'I'm not sure how long the shoot will last.'

'How late will you be?' my father asked immediately.

'I told you, it's hard to say.'

'Well you should at least try to make it back by dinner,' he said. There was an edge to his voice.

'What if I can't make it?' came the sharp reply.

Soon their voices sizzled louder than the eggs frying in the saucepan.

'Don't you work late when you have to?' snapped Mother.

'Yes, but—'

'But it isn't the same for me. Is that it?'

'It's not so black and white. There's a right time for everything. We have children to take care of.'

'I'm twenty-five years old; I've been singing since I was five. This is all I know how to do. If not now, then when is the right time for me?'

'It's not like you don't sing. You have music lessons every week.'

'Listen to you. I'm supposed to be happy with only my lessons? Why don't you just put a leash around me?'

'That's not fair.'

'Just say it. You think this is a hobby, not a career.'

'Bloody hell!' shouted my father, 'Don't pretend like you don't know what I'm talking about.'

'Bullshit!' screamed Mother, 'Every single day I have to deal with your bullshit.'

'You're calling our life bullshit?'

'I'm calling my life bullshit.'

'So you hate your life?'

'I just want to sing. Why won't you let me?'

'That is not true! You have one of the best gurus coming in twice a week to train you. You have your television programmes—'

She cut him off. 'I don't need any more training. And I don't want to do small-time television shows for ever. I want stage shows, my own albums, movie soundtracks. I want to tour the world. All the real stuff.'

'Nothing will ever satisfy you,' my father said bitterly, throwing a half-eaten piece of toast back onto his plate.

'You fell in love with my music,' she said, suddenly lowering her voice.

My father cradled his head in his hands for a minute before angrily pushing his chair backwards. It screeched loudly against the grey cement floor, dropping his blazer from its back. He picked up the blazer and rushed towards the door.

'Go! Escape! Run away and leave me in hell,' my mother yelled at his retreating back. Then she turned to us. 'You girls aren't growing up to be singers. Or *anything* for that matter. I'll see to that.'

Naveen and I both raised our lowered heads. The woman who sat before us was a fire goddess. There was fire coming out of her eyes and ears and mouth, even her hair looked ablaze in the morning sunlight. We must have looked stunned.

'Don't look at me like that,' she said, 'You are girls and girls ought to get married. God knows marriage is the death of an artist.'

There was a shuffling noise as Amol came in with a plate full of eggs, sunny side up. He had been waiting near the door, unsure of when to make his entrance. The minute he placed the eggs on the table, mother picked up her fork and stabbed the egg sitting in the middle of the plate, making it leak yellow goo everywhere. My sister and I sat helplessly, unwilling to eat the sullied eggs but too afraid to leave the table.

Every time I look back on that morning, my mind tends to skip over the screams and tears and hurtful words, coming to rest on the image of a sodden eggy mess. It makes me wish that my parents could have been gentler to each other. It makes me wish that we could have all had our eggs that morning, together, cheerfully, sunny side up.

Even though Mother made it clear that she no longer benefitted from her lessons, she nevertheless continued to take them. Her zeal and dedication for Guru Azim Khan and his every instruction were evident in the very way she looked at him, nodded frequently when he spoke, lowered her eyes when she sang for him, blushed in silence when he smiled at her or crumbled under his judicious stare. On Sundays, she let me and Tilat accompany her to Azim Khan's house as we were close in age to Zubair and Amina, his two children. On these days, Azim Khan's wife squatted in front of their woodfire stove and cooked lunch while Mother finished her lesson and Zubair, Amina, Tilat and I played on their expansive roof. We made a little makeshift kitchen out of cardboard boxes and played a game of pretending to be street-food vendors. We found discarded clay pots, which we filled with water. We ripped heart-shaped leaves from moneyplant creepers and slipped them into the water-filled pots, one by one, making sizzling sounds with our tongues, pretending to fry samosas and parathas in boiling hot oil. By the time the adults ushered us inside for real food, we were dirty, sunburnt and exhilarated.

Inside the Khans' home, however, it was hard not to notice the strict order of things. Our unruly games were not allowed inside. We had to take off our shoes, wash our hands and feet and speak softly. Amina's mother stood erect and monitored our every movement. She stood guard until every morsel of food had been wiped off our plates. Watching her clear the table afterwards, her husband would smile at her benevolently, sending a rush of colour to her cheeks. We called her Khan Auntie, unwittingly destroying the last shred of her identity but she never seemed to mind. The compliant tone of her voice, the forever-upturned corners of her mouth, the way her able hands produced magnificent feasts out of meagre means – it was all as if she lived to please and placate.

Still, it was Khan Auntie's warm laughter and delightful meals that brightened up those Sundays. We did not dare tell Mother, but we were petrified of Azim Khan. His face was eternally puckered up in a rude sneer. His sardonic jokes about how spoiled her children were did not seem to bother our mother but they made us shrink further and further away from him. As the years passed and I became more attuned to his sarcasm, I heard him make many startling remarks to my mother. He brought his small mouth close to her ears and spoke softly, meaningfully, with minimum consideration and maximum impact.

According to her beloved guru, my mother was never quite ready to present her music to the world. The lessons continued in earnest but she never became the star pupil or even the capable student. Before every lesson, Mother pored over her music notes, trying to master whatever assignment had been given to her. But Azim Khan had successfully planted in her the ever-growing seed of self-doubt. She never felt satisfied with her own efforts, just as he expected her not to.

'I need more practice . . .' she'd murmur, voice trailing, eyes glazing.

'Yes you do,' Azim Khan would say, chest swelling with conviction, 'Forget about all those awards you won as a young girl. They mean nothing. You have a long way to go.'

His words not only stunted her growth and clouded her hopes but also crushed the pride and glory of her former years. To my astonishment, Mother never protested. All the spunk with which she fought her husband and disciplined her children vanished when Azim Khan spoke. I watched them, facing each other across the body of the harmonium, mirthlessly practising ragas. He almost gave her a real opportunity once. Or did he only pretend to? He asked her to prepare a song he had composed for the soundtrack of a Bengali feature film. This was to be her big break, a debut into the higher echelons of the music world. This act of uncharacteristic kindness came without warning, which perhaps in itself should have been a sign, but not for Mother. I had never seen such unbridled joy in her. Night after night, she stayed awake and practised the song. She even gave us the rare privilege of listening to her and offering our critiques. Then came the day she was to present the product of her untiring toil to Azim Khan.

'You're not ready,' he said, the familiar words flying out of his mouth as soon as she had finished her song. It was as if he knew all along what he was going to say, except this time those words were meant to squash her one last time, stamp the life out of her like a cockroach under his foot. Just that once, Mother came back from Azim Khan's home, closed the door to her room and howled like a wild animal. Naveen, Tilat and I stood outside the door. We took turns pressing our ears to the cold wooden door and peeking through the keyhole.

To yank the scab off of her wound, my mother's guru often boasted to her about the commercial success of the song, which he had assigned to another student. I like to think it was my mother's perseverance that tied her to him for so long. She had a habit of wanting to match her strength against adversity, as if adversity was a person she needed to impress rather than leave.

As single-minded as her, I too was determined to start music lessons, despite all the angst I naturally associated with music and all the disdain that Mother wanted me to associate with it. I finally announced my decision when I was sixteen years old. Without a shred of enthusiasm, and with something bordering on exasperation, Mother suggested that I should, of course, start under the expert tutelage of Azim Khan. I dreaded the prospect but I was so grateful for her permission that I dared not say anything that might change her mind. Besides, I was older now and less impressionable. I'd also had years to acquaint myself with the man who was to be my new guru. I knew his flaws only too well. Perhaps, now, I could understand what Mother had always seen in him that allowed her to be so tolerant of him.

The first few lessons were uneventful. After a month, I had almost stopped bracing myself for the punishing words when Azim Khan scrunched up his pointy nose – as if there was a bad odour in the room – and asked me what I hoped to gain from music.

'It makes me happy,' I said without thinking.

'Oh, really?' he said, the question, lingering not so much in the words as in the deadening look in his eyes.

I held my ground and stared back at him.

'Look,' he said, suddenly relaxing, 'I've always told your mother the truth, so I'm going to do the same with you.'

It was shocking how quickly he changed his tactic, how quickly he went from openly condescending to cold and calculative. He needed me to believe him.

'Do you know what kids like you remind me of?' he was saying.

I shook my head, surprised by how the sharp pitch of his voice betrayed his tranquil features. There were tiny beads of sweat above his thin upper lip. He was trying hard not to let the bitterness spill out of him and into his face and on to the harmonium and down to the very ground beneath our feet.

'You remind me of young green grass, crushed under a rock. You have no hope of sunlight and no place to grow. Your attempts are in vain,' said Azim Khan.

I didn't refute his sweeping verdict. I couldn't. There was a hypnotic quality to his malice, a certain flair and flow to it. This was a man who spent so much time thinking vindictive thoughts that there was eloquence and ceremony in his words. To argue with him would be to try and fight a wild beast with one's bare hands. Not unlike the lion or the tiger, he was always poised to pounce on his opponent, dig his fangs into their powerless flesh and tear them to bits. Eventually, I learned to anticipate the first gleam of attack in his beady eyes, just before he was about to make a vicious remark. I memorised how he swayed his balding head from side to side when he disapproved of something, which was often. I came to imitate, perfectly, the shape of his small, cunning mouth right after something vile had come out of it. Listening to his unkind words was like watching a puppet show where, despite knowing that someone else manipulates the lifeless figures, you watch, spellbound by the puppet's tricks. In later years, when the immediacy of our interactions receded from my memory, a different aspect of his face emerged, penetrating through the mask of harshness I had come to know so well. Deeply embedded in his small features was a vast fear, one that he sought to transfer to others.

I no longer remember how exactly the lessons stopped. There was no finality or grand conclusion to it. The whole enterprise fizzled out like a fire that never quite reached its potential. I can only assume my mother had expected it because she did not say a word about it nor offered to find me a new guru. Our silence on the matter was mutual, impenetrable and absolute. I continued to sing in the bathroom but there was a hush in my voice and a dullness in my movements. It was hard to believe that just the year before the bathroom had been the sanctuary of my dreams, the mirror a glittering reflection of my unfaltering hope and joy.

Two years later, in my college course catalogue, I came across a picture of Shiva Nataraj, the God of Dance. I ran my forefinger along Shiva's raised limbs as I eyed the caption for the class: Indian Classical Dance I. Old yearnings stirred inside. What if I could find a different passion? A passion to replace music in my life, or more correctly, to erase it from my dreams. Was it even possible? Was it worth the trouble? I ended up signing for the class.

It didn't take long to discover that my joints, unlike my voice, were stiff, awkward and resistant. Symmetry and balance were completely missing in my limbs. I could easily carry a rhythm on my lips but had none in my feet. I was drawn to the beauty of the dance but I was running a fool's errand in trying to be a dancer.

The following semester I signed up for Indian Classical Dance II. I couldn't help it. It was the only place where I could hear the ragas again, listen to the high notes of the harmonium, the pulsating beat of the tabla. In dance class, I could be near those sweet, beloved sounds and try to let my feet do what my voice had always wanted to do.

In the beginning, my senses were mollified. The dynamic between a guru and disciple, combined with the familiarity of the music we danced to, comforted me enough to think that I might have found a new interest, one that would take away the hankering to sing. Every morning I stared at the small dancing figure of Shiva I had picked up from an Indian store and reminded myself that the very God of Dance would help me. My recalcitrant limbs were not as easily convinced but I believed they would ultimately catch up. They had to.

Slowly, I let the idea of dancing seep into me. Because it was supposed to save me from singing, I sought a new, more solid identity in it. I stayed after class and commanded my sore, overworked feet to master the moves. I was too old, my body too inflexible to learn how to do a split or spin on one leg but I tried so hard that by the end of dance class I had no energy left to finish assignments for other classes. Rain or shine, I turned up for dance class, clutching my ankle bells, my body aching with hope. Every day I hoped to find the kind of bliss I'd found in front of the bathroom mirror, holding my pretend pencil microphone. Every day I was disappointed.

By the end of the year, I no longer went to dance class for the love of the ragas or in search of a new passion or even the longing to be delivered from music in the same way that one prays to be delivered from evil. I went because I had let loose a hunger in me, a blind and brutish hunger which proliferated in the perpetual absence of satisfaction. I had felt the first pang of this unrelenting hunger when, on that sweltering afternoon years ago, my friend Raqib and I had kissed and violated our fasts. I waited, ravenously, for the end of each dance practice, when my muscles were too tired to hold me upright, for only then, I was too numbed to feel the roar of that vicious hunger. Dance allowed me to survive by pulverising my body and anesthetising my spirit. Dance had become my saviour, my nemesis.

I was not a talented dancer but my tenacity alone made my teacher offer me a position in the small dance company she ran locally. The hours of dance practice tripled. Now that my teacher had a vested interest in me, she was no longer tolerant of my half splits and slow spins. 'Oye! What's wrong with you? You look like a Shiva with a broken leg. Lift your leg higher, higher, higher . . .' she'd holler at me constantly. On the company T-shirt I wore was, once again, the picture of the same dancing Shiva, balanced on one leg, furiously dancing the universe into creation. Every muscle in my body felt the tautness of his incredible split, every cell of my being felt the tumult of his tandava, that thunderous dance, its explosive thrust, but I could not dance it. No matter how hard I prayed to Shiva Nataraj for a dancing boon, he was as silent and unreadable as the god of my childhood.

My mother's reaction to my newfound occupation further unglued me. 'That's wonderful,' she said emphatically. 'You must continue to dance. I'm so happy to hear it.'

'I'm not very good at it,' I admitted to her.

'So? You'll get better. Just stick with it.'

What I would have given to hear her say that when I gave up my music lessons.

'I wish I could resume my music,' I ventured, emboldened by her enthusiasm.

'Hmmm . . .' she said. This time her voice was barely audible.

One afternoon after dance practice my teacher invited me to join her for a cup of tea. I was almost certain that she would fire me from the company. We drove down the narrow streets of Amherst in her black Toyota Camry until we arrived at a small Asian teahouse. We ordered Chinese tea in a round white teapot with blue and red dragon motifs and tiny matching cups. I sipped the pale tea, trying to identify the scent of the flower in it. A student at the next table was reading a book that caught my eye. It was called *The Wisdom of No Escape*. I wanted to lean over and ask her the name of the author but my teacher spoke first.

'Are you OK?' she asked, her brow creased with concern.

'Yes. Why?' She had caught me off guard.

'Well I've noticed how low you've been lately and I wanted to talk about it.'

I was annoyed. Why not just tell me that dance wasn't for me? I knew it, she knew it. There was no need for Chinese tea or looks of concern. She pulled something out of her handbag and shoved it into my hands. It was a pair of red fleece mittens.

'I've seen that you never wear gloves even when it's freezing cold. I thought these might help,' she smiled, kindly, the way she often did when I was able to only half-perform a difficult move. But she had gone to an awful lot of trouble to simply release me from my own shortcomings. Through the open window of the teahouse, I could see some students lying on a patch of grass, soaking up the late fall sun. Maybe I ought to lie on the grass sometime. Maybe I ought to read a romance novel with the sun on my back, instead of chasing after dancing deities. Maybe I could ask my teacher for help.

'I never wanted to dance,' I said, almost under my breath.

My teacher popped a round red bean cake into her mouth and nodded slowly.

'I wanted to sing,' I said a little louder.

'So why don't you?' she asked.

'I need a teacher.'

'That'll be hard here but I know a lot of people in this town. Do you have some training?'

'Only a little.'

'I'll look around,' she said. 'Let's go, I'll drop you off at school.'

I picked up my backpack and slipped on my warm new mittens. My fists looked cartoonish and I grinned looking at them, realising at the same time that I wasn't going to get fired.

My teacher was resourceful. She gave me the name and number of a Bengali graduate student at UMass who lived in a remote part of the town of Amherst. To get to his house, it would take me an hour and a half from Mount Holyoke and I'd have to change buses three times. The lessons began in the dead of winter. I read my textbooks on the bus and took notes for papers and quizzes. Some days I almost forgot why I was travelling on those lonely New England roads, the snow piled high on either side, giving the impression of rolling through a white tunnel. Beyond the roads, gnarled shapes rose in the silent darkness.

The music teacher was polite and mild-mannered but not exactly a gifted vocalist or even a spirited coach. He was a student himself and was as tired as me when we met on those wintry evenings so that he always seemed to be in a rush to get the lesson over with. In the next room, separated by a thin wall, I could hear his wife and baby girl, shifting, pacing, listening, waiting for him to finish. Often I felt the same lack of mirth I had seen in my mother years ago. Where was the joy, the giddy heights of pleasure I experienced in front of the bathroom mirror? On those icy nights I could not get back to college before 11 p.m. For dinner, I'd raid the vending machine and fall asleep with my coat on, a half-eaten bag of Cheetos next to me.

I would've kept doing everything I was doing to keep my fantasies alive – my fantasies of a singing career, fantasies that scurried under the bed in the presence of my mother and father. My new teacher, however, put an unmanageable price on his lessons. I could not afford an extra $400 every month from my campus job alone, which was my only source of income. My father gave me money for books each semester but I was responsible for the rest of my bills. Asking my father for the additional expense of music lessons was out of the question. His feelings on the subject of music were less ambivalent than my mother's. He had made it clear that music was not an acceptable goal. To make matters worse, the small harmonium I'd brought from home broke down. Without warning it withdrew its music from me. I pressed the keys but no sound came out. 'It froze,' said my teacher. 'These delicate instruments don't do well in this cold weather, you know. I guess we have to wait until next semester before you can go home and get a new one.' He looked relieved.

I was relieved too. For more than two years, I had lived on the fringes of a normal college life. My off-campus dance and music practice, the increased work hours to pay for the music lessons and the hours I spent travelling on buses barely left me enough time to attend classes and do schoolwork. I was always dog-tired. I never went to parties or dinners or dates. I missed important guest speakers and concerts and sports events. I had no time to participate in any of the social or political activism on campus. I was lucky if I could catch a meal at the cafeteria with the few friends I had. So relief it was, but it was the kind of relief that might come from amputating a bad limb.

The day I went for my last lesson was breezy and cool. I saw the first crocuses as I walked from my teacher's house to the bus stop and their feeble heads reminded me of a comment made long ago: *Young green grass, crushed under a rock.* I laughed, the words sounding more ludicrous than cruel after all these years. A homeless man sleeping on a bench looked up at the sound of my laughter. I gave him a quarter.

And I kept on dancing. I twirled and swirled, feeling the world spin off balance, an unsung song on my lips. What drove this feckless compulsion? Was it because my mother approved of dance or was it because she wouldn't approve of music? It was no less wretched than my childish need to polish the world into perfection.

After I graduated from college and moved to New York I had many more options to take music classes. But the number I dialled was of the Indian dance company not the music school I had found. Once again, oddly enough, I was accepted, despite a rather average audition.

'You've got great eyes and perfect hips. Your muscles, um, need more training and time,' said the woman who ran the company. An audition passed on the merit of my eyes and hips. Fate was persistent on giving me a second chance with dance when it had done nothing to help with my music.

My life fell into the old cycle of work, practice and exhausted sleep. The demands of this dance company were much more rigorous than the previous one. My weeknights and weekends were spent rehearsing in a small Manhattan studio on the west side of the city. I hardly had time to explore New York or make new friends. Sometimes, after practice, I went to a bleary diner called Moonlight with my fellow dancers. It was the only social activity I looked forward to. Besides, I was constantly in pain. From overworking my inflamed, intractable joints, I developed an excruciating and chronic back pain. My swollen knees buckled when I climbed up and down stairs. I refused to seek medical help in fear that I might be instructed to stop whatever was aggravating the pain. I spent my entire first year in the city at either my office desk or a dance studio.

At the end of my first New York year, my mother came to visit me. That summer, I was to have my first public recital with the dance company. We were going to perform at the Lincoln Center, three nights in a row. My mother insisted on coming to the show, even though I did my best to convince her that it wouldn't be worth her time. She waved me away. 'I wouldn't miss it for the world,' she said, adamantly.

On the afternoon of my opening performance, she brushed and tied my hair the way she used to when I was little. It always hurt when she ran the comb through my long, tangled masses and as a little girl I'd always cried and complained through the ordeal. When I was a bit older and I learned to braid my own hair, I missed those few minutes when I had her to myself, the way her fingers felt on my scalp, smooth and supple, just before the sharpness of the comb scratched my skin. Now, after a decade, she had offered to braid my hair again. After she finished, she surveyed her work. 'Your curls are softer, straighter,' she said, 'not heavy and tangled like they used to be. I liked the way they were before.'

'Did you?' I asked. 'But you told me you shaved my head seven times in the hope that my hair would grow more straight.'

'When did I say that?' Mother looked piqued.

'You told me that every time I asked you why my head was being shaved.'

'I don't recall. It must have been due to the heat!'

'Mother, it is always hot in Dhaka.'

She sighed, then whispered a prayer under her breath and blew into the hollow of my neck for good luck.

In the dressing room, minutes before the show was about to start, I sat with the other dancers, feeling conspicuous in my overdramatised make-up and glaring silk costume. I kept biting off bits of my freshly painted nails, something I'd never done before. One of the girls came over and placed a hand on my shoulder. 'Nervous?' she smiled. I told her that my mother was out in the audience, waiting to see me dance for the first time.

'You'll make her proud,' my friend said, gently.

It struck me then that I didn't need my mother to be proud of my dance. I needed her to be proud of *me*, me as I was, behind the make-up, under my skin. Waiting in the darkness of the wings, trying to keep still so the bells on my feet wouldn't jangle, I was overcome by a sudden compulsion. I wanted to quietly exit the wings, slip off my silk costume, discard my heavy silver jewellery and scrub my face clean of its garish make-up. Without the protective mask and shield of my dancing gear, I wanted to approach my mother and rest my tired head on her lap. I wanted to tell her that I didn't want to dance, not even for her. But the curtains lifted, the MC spoke into the microphone, the stage filled with light. I whirled out of the wings, trying to summon the rage of Shiva's tandava. On the third row, I spotted my mother. She was leaning noticeably forward in her seat, her shoulders rolled frontward with tension, her hands tightly clasped under her chin. She looked as if she was ready to catch me, should I fall. I didn't quite fall but my eyes glazed, my head reeled and my lumbering feet felt heavier and more awkward than ever before. I knew this was my worst dance to date but I didn't care. This was not my tandava, it would never be. The only universe I had ever created with this dance was a fallacy, a complete fiction.

If my mother thought my dance was awful, she never said a word. Not that I had expected otherwise. I was well acquainted with her reserve on matters that most required her attention. We went out for Mexican food afterwards and she lavished praise on the chicken and spinach burritos. In the dim light of the restaurant I saw shadows dancing on her heart-shaped face. I can never forget her face that night – so familiar, so appealing and so inscrutable – the face of a beloved stranger.

On Report Card Days I wake up without the aid of an alarm clock. Despite the gusto of the ceiling fan, the bed sheets cling to my hot, clammy skin. I can still feel the sharp sting of nightmares behind my eyelids. The grey and white school uniform, starched and ironed, lies across the chair in threatening silence. I have nowhere to hide. The first person I see when Father and I walk in through the school gates is my friend Nadia. On Report Card Days, Nadia's tall frame stands taller, a huge grin across her usually serious face. She clutches the Report Card to her chest like a newborn baby. This is her day and the Report Card is her badge of honour, written evidence of her worth.

For me, this day carries the horrors of Judgement Day, just the way Hujur had described. I run for refuge, but find none. It feels exactly as if I am disintegrating but not quite dying.

'She just doesn't seem to get numbers,' says my maths teacher, 'She's doing well in other classes . . .'

'But a failing grade?' my father gasps.

'Yes, she's in trouble, no doubt,' my teacher confirms.

I see the slash of red ink across the white Report Card. Red indicates a failing grade but it fails to make an impression on me. What draws me is the story behind that number and how my teacher cannot see that story. I'm looking through the exam papers – there they are, the heavily marked sheets where I had walked along parallel lines, danced around in circles, climbed up the sides of triangles, slid down the slopes of hexagons and landed squarely on my face. Even infinity is a loop, it has no opening, no pathway to freedom. Enclosed spaces. Claustrophobia. Doors closing. *You're a girl. You cannot sing.* The shapes entrap me, the numbers limit me; I desperately want a way out. How can I explain this to my father?

Father is talking to my maths teacher, Mr Hossain, jotting down his address. Mr Hossain will coach me over the weekends to rescue me from the deep well of ignorance I have fallen into. He doesn't know. He doesn't know that between the measured spaces of those shapes, lines and numbers, I see the shadowy pauses of my life: my father, sitting cross-legged, shoulders slumped, stale blue smoke stagnant above his head; my mother, young, fiery, a bitter song on her lips; my father sitting at his empty desk stunned that he has been fired; my mother forcing a smile; my father lying on a white hospital bed, half-paralysed, my mother arranging the rows of medication on the nightstand; and myself, unsure, lurking, looking for a glimpse of light that might end these shadowy pauses and play our lives forward again. In these spaces we are stuck, all of us, the angles of our hearts at odds with each other. The red ink on the Report Card is bright as blood, and beneath it, the stories of battles fought and lost, wounds open and raw. It is simply the story of my life written in red.

On the way home, I am waiting for my father to take a closer look at the Report Card, to see the small victories that were there too. I see his eyes scanning the piece of paper. I want him to tell me what he is feeling, even if it is only disappointment. I want him to tell me I am neither stupid nor lazy, want him to hug me, to scold me and to let me hide my head in the musky warmth of his chest. I want him to look at me and see *me* – undefined by those numbers and marks and grades – me as I am, my body, small and thin and crouched in fear. But just like Mother he looks through me and says nothing. His eyes grow cloudy, his lips droop and his cheeks sag. He hands the Report Card back to me and rubs his hands together as if they hurt.

When I was in fifth grade, my efforts to please my father on Report Card Day finally bore some fruit. I came third in my class and won an obese paperback edition of the latest Oxford English Dictionary as my prize. The first and second prizes were storybooks but I was secretly more pleased with the dictionary since I had no shortage of books. Besides, it would only be a matter of time before I'd be reading those very books, since my friend Nadia (who was in first position again) and I swapped books on a weekly basis. We lived just a block away from the school at the time, so I shoved my dictionary into my schoolbag and sprinted home to share the news of my accomplishment. Father was sitting on his cane chair in the balcony, reading a copy of *Newsweek*, holding a mug of tea in his free hand. He looked up and I held out the dark-blue and green striped dictionary on outstretched palms. He took the book, flipped open the front cover and read the designation: Third Prize/Maria Chaudhuri/Based on Meritorious Academic Performance. I held my breath for the embrace or the exclamation that would surely follow. I squeezed my eyes closed and opened them again just in time to catch the veil of disappointment that darkened my father's brow before he caught himself and turned it into a wan smile.

'Not bad,' he said, 'but this means you can do even better. If you can be in the top three, you can be at the very top.' He handed the dictionary back to me and went back to his reading.

Slowly, I walked back to my room and placed the dictionary on the topmost rack of the book shelf. I couldn't bring myself to break its delicate spine, to disturb its beauty and solitude for the mere purpose of finding the meanings of words. For me, that dictionary preserved more meaning than words ever could. Within its untouched pages it hid both my pride and my shame – an intense burst of childish pride

forever tarnished by the all too quick onslaught of an insurmountable shame.

My father and I never really spoke about the pulsating
tension of those Report Card Days. If he spoke to me at all it
was usually to enquire about schoolwork. This hardly led to
full-fledged conversations though sometimes Father decided
to turn his enquiry into a lecture about my sister Naveen's
superior academic performance. Baffled and resigned at the
news of yet another mediocre grade from me, he'd ask me,
'You are sisters, born of the same parents, nourished with the
same love and care. Then why is it so hard for you to achieve
what she does so easily?'

I turned to Naveen for answers. After all, she was smarter
than me, she would know what I didn't. 'What do you think
I'll be good at when I grow up?' I asked her coyly.

'How should I know?' she said, shrugging. 'Maybe
gardening?'

'That's not funny.'

'Well, what do you want me to say? That you'll grow up to
be a scientist?'

'Maybe I'll be a singer, like Mother,' I retorted.

Naveen sniggered, then looked at me pitifully.

Naveen was about to graduate from Yale with an impres-
sive double major in Economics and Mathematics just as I
was getting ready to graduate from high school. My days
passed in constant agony over the prospect of not getting
admission into an American institution like Naveen. I did not
hope for Yale, nor did I want it. I wanted a clean slate. Though
I've forgottenthe exact words, I wrote something to this effect
on every college essay:

What I want is a place where I can explore and discover
and build my own dreams. A place to get to know myself.
What I want is a new home.

I sealed every application package with a heartfelt prayer,
except the one for Yale. It was the one place where I could not
start anew, yet it was the one achievement that might have
redeemed me in my father's eyes. It was a warm midsummer's
day when the mailman walked up our block with a large envelope from Mount Holyoke College bearing my name on it. I
snatched it from his startled hands and ran to the bathroom. I
hugged the envelope to my chest and breathed in the foreign
smell of its contents. I pulled out the brochure inside and
surveyed every picture in it. I imagined myself lying on the
sprawling campus green, face up, taking in the vast New
England sky. A week later, another admission letter arrived
from the University of Chicago but I had already planted my
heart in an idyllic little town in Western Massachusetts,
tucked away by the Connecticut River. Though it fell outside
the bounds of fact or logic, they were, in my mind, the first
people to accept me as I was.

Nothing could have prepared me for my father's reaction to
the news of my college admission. I had fully expected a
disquieting speech on the ordinariness of my accomplish-
ments in comparison to Naveen's. Why even bother going all
the way to America if it was just to attend an ordinary school?
All non-Ivy League schools were ordinary in my father's
opinion. How many times had I heard him tell his friends,
chest puffed out, eyes shining, that his eldest daughter was a
Yalee? He had learned that swanky term and dropped it into

conversations with casual abandon. But as he held my letter in his hands, inspecting it carefully, he neither smiled nor grimaced. When he looked up, his tone was soft, his shoulders stooped a little.

'OK, you've proved that you can do it. Now will you stay here in Dhaka?'

I gulped. What had I proved? Was he barring me from going to America because I had let him down yet again?

'Where would I go to college?' I was finding it hard to speak.

'Right here in Dhaka. It's not the end of the world you know. There are good schools here too.'

'You don't think Mount Holyoke is a good school?' I dreaded the answer but I had to know.

'Of course it is. That's why I said you have proved yourself.'

'Then why can't I go?'

'I didn't say you can't. I asked you if you might want to stay.'

My apprehension was slowly turning into confusion. There was something different about the way my father spoke. There was a plea in his voice, a sadness in his posture. In the pale light of late afternoon, I could barely see his eyes but I thought they glistened with moisture. It took me way too many wasted years to acknowledge that exchange as my father's first and last attempt to tell me that he loved me. However I was, whatever it was that I could never be, he still wanted me right there by his side, inside the circle of our family, within the four walls of our home, for as long as we were alive. That was love. But I didn't allow myself to see it just then. Contrary to what my father thought, I didn't feel like I had proved myself at all. I hadn't even begun to. And I didn't know then, but I would never have the chance to begin.

Later, it was Shonali who described to me what had happened the night I left Dhaka. Upon his return from seeing me off at the airport, my father had gone straight to the roof where he sat down on one of the broken plastic chairs and waited alone in the dark. We lived close to the airport, so when the airplanes flew over our home, they were still low in the sky and easily seen, even their logos discernible on a clear night. I have no way of knowing whether it was really my plane or a different one that flew over our roof and found my father suddenly on his knees, his thin frame jerking spasmodically as he used the back of his palms to wipe away the tears that kept his eyes from following the last trace of the airplane.

But the heart rebukes us as much as it gives us joy. It allows for only as much glory as can be countered by punishment. If my father could have cut his heart open, or even given me an itty-bitty slice of it, we could have had our glory and foregone the punishment. In subsequent weeks, when I picked up the phone and called my father across the Atlantic Ocean, his voice sounded flat, resigned. It reminded me of his drooping face as he handed me back my Report Cards. In the typical fashion of the previous years, our conversations settled into the dismal drill of exchanging information on my academic progress, the status of my bank account and tuition bills. As far as the mind could fathom, I was, to Father, a duty to be fulfilled, a duty he would never abandon, but a duty nevertheless.

How I longed to tell him about all the new people I had met, the new things I was learning. Did he know I had signed up for a Religion class and was deep into the throes of a life-long fascination with Buddhism? Should I tell him about the poisonous cafeteria food that had me on a staple diet of coffee and bagels? Would he perhaps care to know that my room-mate from Kansas had locked me out of the room and reported me to the Resident Student Advisor because I invited too many boys into it? I searched my brain for things to ask my father. Did he still stay in touch with the pir? Had he visited his older sister recently, was she still in the hospital with kidney problems? But whatever question I came up with seemed paltry, unimportant. Had I never chatted with him? Certainly the need for it had not pressed down on us as hard as it did, when we sat restlessly mute, each at the receiving end of a voiceless machine.

My frustration imploded in recurring nightmares in my sophomore year in college when my father suddenly passed away. I often saw him framed in a ghoulish light, pale with fury. With the speed of rage, my father chased me through dark hallways and deserted streets. His head seemed unusu-ally large, his skin a withered grey and his teeth a sickly yellow. Sometimes he grunted like an animal when he got close to me but I always managed to escape him. Sometimes he didn't chase me at all but sat at the foot of my bed and stared at me with red, accusing eyes.

One night he brought his face close to mine as if to bite me and I woke up to the sound of my own cry. There was a pres-sure on my lower abdomen. I started for the bathroom and in the darkness I thought I saw a man's silhouette, standing still, waiting. What was he waiting for? *Rest in peace, Father*, I said under my breath, *please rest in peace.*

Sometimes my mother asked if I ever dreamed about him. I could not bring myself to tell her how frightful Father seemed in my dreams so I told her that I had seen him floating about in white garments, serene and stoic, like those in Heaven must be.

'He is watching over you,' Mother concluded.

I did not know if my father was watching over me but I knew those dreams came to reconcile me with truths I had not accepted. My father was not coming back to erase the longing he had left in me. And yet, I had withheld from my father the same assurances he had kept from me. He wanted me to summon the genie of the magic lamp and become a poster child overnight. No more the day-dreaming, bathroom-singing, novel-reading, number-hating, gawky child. He wanted me to perk up, focus, add up the numbers and get the answer right, because, to him, there was only one right answer. In my turn, I never did look him in the eye to tell him that I would at least try to do things his way. Perhaps, because, I doubted that I ever could.

My father had a white car, a 1969 Toyota Corolla that he bought the same year he married my mother. Mother always said that the car was his first love and she wasn't too far from the truth. There is an old sepia photograph of my older sister, ten months old, held upright on the hood of the car by a radiant Father. The car was then almost two years old but it looked brand new. Our patience and good feelings towards the car ran out about ten years after its introduction into our family. We wanted to live up to the times, keep up with the Jones's. Not Father. He would not hear of buying a new car. 'This car is in perfect condition,' he insisted every time one of us broached the subject.

Part of the reason the car was in such perfect shape was because Father hardly allowed us to use or even touch it. He laid down the rules: No leaning against the car. No eating or drinking in the car. No loud music in the car. Car would not enter any narrow streets or crowded areas (how was this possible in a city like Dhaka?) Car could not be driven above the speed of sixty kilometres an hour. Car could not be driven by anyone but himself and most certainly not by a paid driver. Rickshaws were to be used for journeys under thirty minutes and baby-taxis for longer trips. The last rule made Mother so angry that she often turned down invitations and refused to go anywhere. 'What madness is this? Do we have a car or an invalid?' she'd scream, and rightfully so.

My father was as solid as a rock in his resolution to preserve the car as one might a family heirloom. It was at first funny, then annoying, and ultimately an embarrassment. Each time there was a friend's birthday party or a lunch or dinner we'd have to ask other friends for a ride. Even going to school or out to shop became a nuisance. We were perpetually at other people's mercy or suffering through the hazards of Dhaka public transportation, despite the shining white (ancient) car supine in our garage, like Sleeping Beauty. We gave it up and went about our business, my father being incorrigible when it came to his beloved car.

One evening, Father agreed to pick up some sweets from a neighbourhood store as we were expecting guests. He let me come with him. On our way back, we saw, about fifteen feet ahead of us, the slow progression of a mob. In Dhaka, political rallies and public protests were routine scenes. They were carrying banners and flags and the people in the front lines were chanting loud slogans that the whole procession zealously repeated after them. Traffic was halted as the mob filled the expanse of the street. Cars honked impatiently, knowing full well that on Dhaka roads, it was far more important to endure the workings of an excited mob than the breaking of traffic rules. Then again, if fate ever was tempted it was on the streets of Dhaka. As the crowd slowly passed the line of vehicles and came nearer, another irritated round of honking rose from some of the cars. In the blink of an eye, a young man wearing a bandanna unclasped a hockey stick from his waistband and brandished it at one of the cars. Before he had finished breaking the windshield of that car, a few other men unclasped their hockey sticks as well.

I watched the scene unfold with rapturous attention until I heard a strange rasping noise and turned to see father clutching the steering wheel, trying to gulp air as if it were his last breath. I was sure he was having a heart attack. 'What is it?' I asked him again and again but he couldn't respond. What was I to do? I looked back at the crowd and saw, thankfully, that some kind of negotiation was already underway. Many drivers had stepped out of their cars and two traffic policemen appeared out of nowhere. 'Father, look, it's going to be fine,' I said hopefully.

He shook his head. 'My car,' he whispered finally, 'they could've hurt my car.'

I touched his shoulder lightly. Sweat was dripping profusely from his scalp, down his neck and shoulders, but his breathing was slowly returning to normal.

'The car is fine,' I said gently.

Someone honked behind us and I realised that the crowd had been streamlined to one side of the street and cars were being allowed to pass. 'Go!' I yelled and Father clutched the gear, shaking uncontrollably. I kept a hand on his shoulder all the way home. I was not sure if the physical touch helped him or if he even noticed it but that was the closest I ever came to showing my fondness for my father.

The distance between my father and me, the unbearable, unconquerable distance that perpetually kept us apart, was fraught with veneration and curiosity. I saw him briefly in the mornings, wearing dark suits and silk ties. In the evenings, he headed out for a game of tennis in a white polo shirt and white sneakers. On nights and weekends, he filled a glass with beer or whisky and got to work. He wrote and wrote, his meticulous handwriting filling yellow notepads, which he carefully tucked away in his black leather briefcase. Opening his briefcase when he was elsewhere was a forbidden pleasure. It was cool and neat inside, with the crisp smell of all things foreign, since the briefcase diligently went around the world with Father. The pens, pencils and paper he kept inside were so different from the ones we bought from the local stores that I often felt compelled to steal an item or two as souvenirs of his adventures. Adventures I imagined he had. Those items hinted at the stories my father never had time to tell.

If he wasn't working, he seemed preoccupied with being productive in other ways. His clothes, after being washed and ironed, were left on his bed, as he preferred to put them away in the exact arrangement he favoured. If it were only up to my father, undoubtedly our home would have been as pristine as the inside of his briefcase or closet. He always walked with his eyes down, scouting the floor for dirt, picking up strands of hair, brushing imaginary dust off every conceivable surface. His usually peaceful demeanour was liable to be incensed by the slightest disruption of orderliness.

There was one task my father undertook that I looked forward to. On wintry Sundays, he sat peeling dozens of oranges that he lovingly distributed among us. Even though the orange is not my favourite fruit, I am still inexplicably drawn to its shape and colour, because it reminds me of the only elaborate show of fatherly warmth, on those lazy Sundays, when Mother and the four of us sprawled on the sun-dappled veranda floor while Father sat on his white cane chair with a basket of oranges and a sheet of newspaper on his lap. Other than oranges, however, Father was strangely repulsed by the flesh and seed of all other fruits and mindlessly swooped down on our half-eaten fares to fling them into the garbage. It made me feel as if he organised our communal orange-feasting more out of his appreciation for that sweet seasonal delight than anything else. Not that I would trade the ritual for anything. When else would I see my father without the silk ties and travel luggage, constantly racing towards something? Something other than us.

The blessed day did arrive though, when I was eight or nine years old, when Mother suggested that we come along on one of Father's trips abroad. She reasoned that it was the only way we would ever take a family trip together. None of us kids had ever been abroad and even if it meant that Father would be working half the time, it was still better than not having a family vacation at all.

We were all for the idea, even though Father seemed indifferent to the plan. He nodded absently when Mother brought it up so we took that to be an affirmative. Naveen and I started planning what we would wear on the airplane. We had been to the airport many times to see Father off and had noticed how well-dressed everyone was, or at least those who were going somewhere. Father, certainly, was always dressed in a suit and cut straight through to the business-class counter that had a shorter queue in front of it. It all seemed very formal and proper. Naveen decided she would wear her Indonesian wraparound skirt with a white blouse, and I, more of a fashion victim than her, decided to wear my orange pantsuit with dark sunglasses.

We knew Father's next trip was to the Philippines and we wondered if that's where we would be going for our much-awaited holiday. We had no idea what any place was like except through the gifts and souvenirs that Father brought back for us. From Manila, he always returned with the most delicious sweets, soft and milky white, creamy and coated with a dusting of sugar. We never tired of them. But one evening, we heard Father telling Mother that it would be best if she met him in Bangkok rather than Manila. Thailand was much more fun than the Philippines and also a shorter flight from Dhaka.

We were giddy with excitement. Bangkok was a popular holiday destination among our friends and we were practically the last kids in our respective classes to be going there. We knew Bangkok had, among other things, huge malls, crowded beaches and spicy, mouth-watering food. We were a little troubled by the fact that we didn't own any beachwear but at least we could go into stores and choose what we liked instead of having Father pick out what we needed.

The morning Father left for Manila, he hugged and kissed each of us goodbye as usual but no other words or instructions were exchanged. We didn't mind. We figured Mother knew what had to be done for the Bangkok trip, which was coming up in a week. A few more days passed and then Mother told Amol to retrieve her green suitcase from the dusty attic. Once Amol placed it on her bedroom floor, she started packing her clothes and cosmetics into it, humming cheerfully the entire time. Naveen and I sat on her bed, watching, waiting for the moment when she would tell us to start packing our things too. I had already packed and re-packed my suitcase a thousand times in my head, so I knew exactly what I was bringing on the trip.

It wasn't until Mother was almost done that we realised we were not going to be packing our things. Because we were not going anywhere. Mother was meeting our father in Bangkok all by herself. 'It's just easier, you know. How can I manage the airplane journey alone with four kids? And your brother is still just a baby.' She smiled kindly. 'Please make your lists. I'll get you whatever you like.'

I remember crying to sleep that night. I remember making a long shopping list in the middle of the night and then tearing it to bits. I remember going to the airport with Mother to see her off and feeling heartbroken all over again. I remember vowing to myself that one day I would travel the world all by myself. But I don't remember my father ever realising how he disappointed us that time or many a time after, when he simply refused to understand what we wanted.

My parents did take a few trips together – not as many as would have satisfied my mother – but our family trip never happened. How I wish it had and not because it would have allowed me to buy all sorts of goodies or swim in the ocean or frequent those delicious eateries that I had only read about in books. I wish it had happened so that I could have removed my father from the everyday canvas of home and work and built a memory with him that was different, so colourfully different, from all the grey ones I have.

The afternoon light begins to wane when my father returns from work, shoulders slumped, head bent, the picture of defeat. This is how he looks, every day, when he returns home from his new job. Slowly, he walks down the narrow hallway, past the kitchen where Amol is arranging tea and biscuits on a wooden tray, past the dining room where I am standing. I watch him step into the bedroom, put his black leather briefcase down and reach to unclasp his wrist watch and that is precisely the moment he falls. My mother is running. So am I, with Amol right behind me. By the time we get to him, my father is on the floor, frozen in shock. He cannot lift himself up, nor can he manoeuvre his left leg or arm. The three of us haul him onto the bed and gently prop his head against the pillows. In the broiling heat, the blood drains from his terrified face. 'It must be the heat,' says my mother, 'you've been out in the sun too long.'

It isn't the heat. It couldn't be, because Father hasn't been out in the sun. Even after my mother places him under the ceiling fan with a cool rag on his forehead and feeds him iced lemonade through a straw, my father's pallor continues to turn sickly and his body more slack. His head drops to one side and he dozes in and out of an exhausted stupor. Mother asks him if he's in pain but he has trouble speaking. The words come out of his mouth in a garbled litter. I see the terror in my father's eyes, reflected in my mother's. I watch her reach for the phone as she retrieves her small phonebook from her handbag. I know I should stay near Mother. I should look for Tilat and Avi, who are somewhere downstairs, playing with the neighbours' kids. Most of all, I need to be here for my father. But I cannot bear the sight of his sallow face, nor the faintly sick fumes of his breath. I turn towards the open windows aware now of the sweet smell of young mango buds drifting in, heralding the beginning of summer. Twilight has painted the skyline scarlet. Yet, tonight, this sweet scent nauseates me. Tonight, the scarlet horizon is nothing but the heavens gushing blood. I am running again, fast and faster, until I reach the precarious tin ledge above our roof, hidden from the view of the world, soundless, except for the beating of my heart. This delicate and demanding heart.

I must have fallen asleep. Amol's voice comes from far away as the squeaking of his rubber slippers halts directly under the ledge. If he hauls himself up to the ledge he will see me lying there, shivering under a full moon. I stay still, wondering which of my parents Amol has brought to my secret hideout.

'Your father is not well,' he says quietly, 'you should come down now.'

The scratchy material of the straw mat under me bristles through my dress. I look up at the diseased moon, its luminous belly bulging with infection. I force myself to sit up straight. As I make my way down the stairs, I hear the sirens of an ambulance.

To anyone looking in from outside, my father, forty-seven years old, fit as a horse, smart, successful and mild-mannered, was not an obvious candidate for an early aneurysm. But nobody knew just how fragile he was, until the stroke made it evident. The brittleness of his nature surfaced sometime after he was fired from the company he had dedicated himself to for ten tireless years. The same company that had robbed us of our family holidays, demanded that Mother's music remain a hobby and left us children feeling as if we were always on a wild goose chase for Father. How many Eids had passed with Father at the office, the white Toyota resting in the garage, and us, sparkling in our new clothes but stuck at home because Mother refused to put on a new sari or take us anywhere without her husband. We would plant ourselves by the window, taking in the festive flow of cars, baby taxis and rickshaws on the street below. Eventually we'd get tired of pretending that we too were going somewhere and settle in front of the television, new clothes neatly folded away. How many birthdays and school plays and summer holidays had passed without a sign of Father? He was always at the same place, devotedly stationary, but never where we needed him to be. This company, the faceless monstrosity that loomed in our lives every day, decided one day to withdraw its trust and dependence from its most faithful member. We heard Mother and Father whispering late into the night. At ten years of age, it was the first time I heard the term 'office politics'. After about a week, my parents stopped whispering and spoke openly of the terrible betrayal that my father had been a victim of. Mother mourned luxuriously and at length. For months on end she deliriously chanted the names of every colleague who had possibly plotted against my father and cursed them wholeheartedly. Then came the season of sorrow. Tears were shed at the drop of a hat, regret and loss oozed from her skin, each day was a painstaking eulogy to the death of a man who was still alive. But she lived her pain, no matter how unbecoming it was. With each lament and every slander, she retrieved her strength and sanity.

Two weeks after Father lost his job, my friend Saba informed me that her parents were about to invite mine to one of their famed social events. These parties hosted the elite of Dhaka – small, close groups of people who clung to each other for reassurance. It had been about a year since Father's company had promoted him to the highest position in all of Asia. The news of his success had travelled beyond the professional realm. Acceptance into and by an inner circle of the city's successful men and women had arrived in the form of a much-coveted invitation.

'You should come along,' said Saba. 'We have so much fun. The parents just sort of forget about us … and we're allowed unlimited Coke and Pepsi. Wear something nice!'

I wasn't so excited about drinking Pepsi and my wardrobe was still wanting but it never crossed my mind that the end of my father's height of success also meant the end of our social selves. Mother politely turned down the invitation and then sternly instructed us not to disclose anything to anyone about our great misfortune. 'When your father finds work again, people will know he changed jobs. Until then, no one must know of what happened.' *What*, indeed, had happened? I had not quite come to grasp how Father's achievements, his very image, defined me in others' eyes. Until then, I had only been aware of how he saw me and what he wanted me to be. Who was I supposed to be now that my father was no longer what he had been?

The story is never as simple as the plot. The plot has a beginning, a middle and an end. The story continues, spilling in all directions, drowning the plot in its tidal wrath. As far as the plot goes, my father loses his job, injures his pride and disappoints himself. Eventually, he finds other jobs, takes care of his family and the rest happens as it might have, under any circumstances. We continue to live in the same house, go to the same school, eat the same food. Inside our story, this is not the case. Inside our story, time is no longer linear, space is no longer tangible. Father's job was his soul's sustenance; the small, square space of his office his only real home. So even though Father met his fate with a dignified silence on the surface, an incurable malignance brewed underneath. It struck me that my father, seemingly patient and self-restrained, had always worn his heart on his sleeve, so much so that it never stood a chance in the face of adversity. Reeling from his loss, we turned our home into a mourning chamber. Like ostriches, we buried our faces in the ground and hoped that no one would notice. Mother stopped throwing dinner parties and we never invited friends over during school breaks in case they saw Father at home in the middle of the day. We did get better at concealing our unspeakable secret. After a few months, if someone called on us, unannounced, the smiles easily rose to our lips, the conversation never missed a beat. But we should not have mourned with such ceremony the loss of Father's worldly feats when in fact his biggest disadvantage was an incapacity to adapt to the world.

* * *

As the years went by, my father's elegant persona took on an aura of melancholy; the strength and precision of his ambitious mind swerved out of focus; the purity of his filial love was obscured by undue expectation, embittered by subsequent disappointments and fuelled forward by duty alone. If my childhood was ablaze with my parents' fiery disputes, it was their mutual, cold and bitter discontent that hung like an ashen haze over my adolescent years.

The year before I left for college, I sat with the humongous SAT prepbook every evening and diligently plodded through the practice tests. Usually, my parents maintained a respectful distance during these sessions. After all, studying was comparable to an act of worship. But that evening, I heard their voices loud and clear, travelling all the way from their bedroom to the dining room where I sat. We had just moved into our own house, a house that my parents had built, brick by brick, with their entire lives' savings, the house that had been among the top three items in the prayer list my father had made for us a very long time ago. Back then, I hardly understood the larger implications of my (forced) daily imploration to the Almighty; what spurred me to pass on the request in the first place was the pledge of a big and majestic home. Of course I wanted my own room, my own bathroom, and yes, a garden too. Spellbound by storybook fantasies of a kingly abode, it never occurred to me – until much later – that for my parents so much more was at stake than mere space and sparkle.

In time, the prayers became more frantic and specific. Please, God, can you give us our dream home by the end of *this* year? By the time I was thirteen, it was a weekly ritual to crowd into our old white Toyota Corolla and drive to the other end of town where my father planned to build our house. Baridhara had been a poor and underdeveloped neighbourhood until the government bought the land and decided to sell it at subsidised prices. Huge bungalow-style mansions were constructed next to shanty homes facing inevitable demolition. Foreign embassies moved their offices to Baridhara, making it a highly secure zone. A winding strip of green with stone benches was fenced off for the classy new residents to enjoy their leisurely strolls around Baridhara Lake where dhopas had washed clothes not too long ago. My sisters and I had memorised every detail of every house in the neighbourhood and we discussed at length how our own house might be even better. My father never spoke much. He wove the car slowly through every street until it grew dark and the windows of the enchanted homes lit up, one by one, like bright stars on a clear night. Reluctantly, he would turn the car around, shaking his head as if he was waking from a marvellous dream.

Ours was a three-storeyed building; the first two floors comprised a beautiful, nine-room duplex and the third floor was a more modest, much smaller apartment. We lived on the third floor, which only deepened the regret of not being able to live in the duplex as had been originally intended. Halfway through the construction of the house, Father's resources had become dangerously depleted. He had not anticipated the loss of his job and although he found other work it was never good enough to restore him to his former glory, financially or emotionally. But the house, a skinny skeletal edifice pushing up under the fragrant shade of a kodom tree, begged for completion. For three long years my parents visited the skeleton every day, gave it their love, pumped their blood into its rock-solid heart and held its hand through every stone and brick and pillar. Those were long years for us. The mantra of our home had changed from surrender to sacrifice.

It was during those unfortunate years that I took it upon myself to demand a bicycle and, thus refused, never again found the spirit to master one in later years. Holidays were already denied to us, but now we lost the annual winter trips to Bagh Bari as well as the numerous treats that Father used to bring back from his trips abroad. At first I felt a sense of duty and did the due diligence that was required of me to take part in such collective sacrifice. As one could only have expected based on her stellar academic career, Naveen received a full scholarship from Yale and left for college soon after construction began on the Big House – as we had come to refer to it – and three years later, when the Big House was almost ready, it was my turn to fly the coop. The very foundation of our family continued to change and yet my parents' only dream was to erect a grand mansion that would keep us together for ever.

So, bit by painful bit, the stone skeleton gathered flesh and came to life. A magnificent white structure now towered above the kodom tree, gleaming under a fluffy autumn sky. And, as always, the Big House put its creators to the test. With a huge bank loan over his head, one daughter in college, three others in school and zero savings, it was quite impossible for us to move into the Big House. To do so would mean living hand to mouth each day as well as jeopardise our school and college prospects. The only thing left to do was rent out the Big House rather than move into it.

I'm not sure whose idea it was to take a further loan from the bank and build the third-floor apartment. It was decided that we would rent out the Big House for a few years and when some of the loan had been paid off and some savings restored, we would move in there and rent out the smaller flat. The decision made no real sense, even to someone as mathematically ungifted as myself. But it was as if both my mother and father had their feet firmly rooted on the very earth that held the founding pillars of their precious home. Father's bank loan increased, tenants moved into Mother's dream home and the six of us moved into the haphazardly designed apartment from where we could peer down at what was but would never be ours.

In time we grew fond of the tenants. Tarun and Lalita were Indian Bengalis who had just moved to Dhaka. The success and glamour of their young lives were apparent in the way they decorated their new home and the grand parties they hosted. We were always invited to their stylish soirées, where I soon discovered that Tarun's eyes were not entirely fixed on his pretty wife. At seventeen, I quite enjoyed the attention, offered over a forbidden glass of wine, and even Mother was charmed by Tarun's sharp humour and Lalita's excellent hospitality. Most of all, Mother was at once incensed and mollified by how beautiful her home (she still called it her home) looked in the company of perfect strangers.

My father still sat in his white cane chair but it had been placed in one corner of the living room, since the balcony in the new apartment was too tiny. With the loss of a sizeable balcony, we lost the orange-feasting rituals on wintry mornings. We might have forgotten about the very existence of the balcony had it not been for the few pots of herbs that Mother had placed along the black iron banister, and only when the evening breeze carried in the enticing scents of basil and mint were we drawn to the little balcony which was but a mockery of the long and expansive terraces of former years. What we missed most, each one of us, was the promise and anticipation of something great, something better. Perhaps we had all hoped, in our own ways, that moving into the Big House, where every object and pattern had been hand-picked by us, would somehow redesign the blueprint of our relationships and restore our faith in what the future held.

'This is what I've lived for? This joke of a home?' came Mother's voice that evening, sharp and sneering, geared to offend.

'People live in worse, much worse conditions,' replied my father, coldly.

'Well, I'm not those people and to think I poured three years of blood and sweat and money into a home where someone else gets to stay. Is there nothing you can do right?'

'Yes, this is all my fault,' Father said after a long pause. There was a dangerous flatness to his voice.

'Everything in this family is your fault. You are incapable of making us happy.'

Although I had witnessed their arguments throughout my life, something about Mother's last words made me catch my breath. I couldn't see their faces but even from a distance I could feel the heartbreak those words were meant to cause. I felt my father flinch and snap. I felt Mother's victory and remorse all congealed into one festering wound. And then I heard the shattering of glass. Before I knew it I was standing before them and I saw my father kneeling at the edge of the bed gasping for breath as he clutched his chest. A few feet across the room Mother stood still, unable and unwilling to traverse the path of splintered glass left by broken tea cups and saucers, the length of the massacred floor distending between them like a bloodied battleground.

We never did move into the Big House, even after Tarun and Lalita left. The black, red and white kitchen with shiny marble-top counters – modelled after one of Mother's home-decor magazines – was buffed and polished for many more tenant families until it began to lose its lustre and newness. The long stretch of balcony where Tarun and Lalita had hung a hammock under our envious eyes grew dark patches on its milky white cement floor with each passing monsoon. More and more high-rises sprang up around our neighbourhood blocking the golden morning light streaming in through the white French windows of the Big House.

From the night of their wedding my parents had been chasing a candlelit room, a beautiful home from where to bring forth the perfect start to their lives. Every time they got close the room vanished, the house crumbled. And they never could begin their lives. So there they were, constantly fighting to get back to the beginning when all they were really doing was stalling the macabre end. For Father, the end came with the final and irrevocable accusation that he could never make us happy. He surrendered to the terrible absolution of this verdict in complete silence, with a perpetually bent head. At all hours of the day and night he slumped in his cane chair or on top of his prayer mat, waiting, always waiting to be released from himself.

* * *

On the day of my father's funeral, I learned a curious thing. We took his body to the cemetery just before sundown to bury him before the evening prayer call. Friends and relatives pooled into several cars to join the funeral procession. At the entrance of the cemetery, my cousin's husband stopped us.

'This is as far as women can come. No woman can be present at the burial site,' he said. Astonished, I turned to Mother, expecting a scathing response from her, but she was backing away, slowly, obediently. I looked to Naveen and Tilat for support but they turned their faces away.

'Why can't women be at the burial?' I asked, at last.

'It's bad luck,' came the firm reply.

We stood outside in the gathering murk, my mother, sisters and I, together with a few other women friends and relatives. I watched helplessly as distant relations and veritable strangers accompanied my brother Avi to perform the last rites for our father. As the men disappeared with Avi, I knew what I had been denied. I'd been denied the last tears – the slow, satiating pain of a final touch, a final word, a final look, a final goodbye. When the prayer call rang out from the city's mosques, we knew that our father had been put to rest in the freshly dug earth. I gazed up at the pink sky, as I had done so many times before, hoping to see the open doorways of Heaven beckon its wandering souls back inside. The other women immediately pulled their dupattas over their heads and cupped their hands in prayer. I wanted, more than anything else, to utter a last prayer for Father. All my life I had defied his wish to see me succumb in ceremonial prayer. And I couldn't raise my hands now to summon a single syllable that was worthy of a last sacrament for him. I watched the intent faces of those whose eyes were still closed in quiet supplication, the sorrow and reverence in their hearts finding form and release in the act of prayer. For the first time in my life I felt the need to be quiet, to pause and fill myself with a presence that was bigger than me. It was a peculiar sensation, euphoric yet calm, searing open a space in the middle of my chest that remained ajar and alight. In a quick and deliberate flash of memory I saw my father, slouching on his prayer mat, tears on his cheeks, eyes far away, lips frozen in a faint smile. Then the image was gone, along with the sensation. Complete darkness descended upon the cemetery and there was not much sound except the intermittent buzzing of crickets.

Later I was told that women were not permitted to be near a burial for two reasons. One was based on the belief that women could be polluted by menstrual blood, which might draw evil spirits near the dead. The other reason struck me as a more arresting one: it had to do with a woman's alleged lack of control over her grief. If she broke down and exposed her deepest sorrow to the departing soul, she made it hard for the soul to leave earth.

I wanted my father to reach whatever destination awaited him after death. I wanted him to find his home in the next life. If there really was another life out there for him then I wanted him to be happy in it, happier than he had been in this one. At the very least, I hoped that death would complete the circle of his life rather than rob him of its meaning. But even if death completed a circle for my father, it only decapitated our family further, decimating the idea of our home.

More than twenty years after all our earnest prayers gave birth to the Big House, I am still in the dark about what home had really meant to my father and mother. Was it simply the amalgamation of a city, a neighbourhood, a street, a few rooms and a garden? Was it only a structure of steel and concrete or was it a gateway to something beyond? And without even fully understanding it I had smeared myself with their restlessness, assigned myself the same thankless task of finding and creating a home that would hide the clutter of my life in its gracefully organised rooms. Worse still, the restlessness slowly turned into a cold determination. I vowed not to let myself get attached to the idea of a home. I sought a kind of home*less*ness – not the kind to land me penniless on the sidewalk – but the kind that would constantly keep me on the move, making it impossible to build a home, to nest, to grow roots. I would spend my life travelling, wandering, moving in and out of new towns and cities.

'Do you think you'll ever return home?' friends have asked me. The question annoys me, mostly because I do not know the answer to it.

'What is home?' I snap. 'Especially in this day and age? Look at this global world we live in.'

'Ah, but everyone has a home . . .' some of them persist, with a touch of pity in their voices.

So I devised, very cleverly I thought, a response to the question of where home might be for me, one that spoke of no partialness to one place or another. Playing on the trendiness of being a truly global citizen, I'd say, with great affectation, 'You see, I want to live in a place that's a perfect blend of the East and the West.' Grunts of sarcasm usually followed such a chimera of implied largesse, though curiosity welled at the thought of this cosmopolitan utopia. 'And what place is that, for you?' Of course I did not know. If I knew, I'd have lived there. I liked the sound of it, could intuit the philosophy of it, but I was only Alice in the Wonderland of my own naiveté. What I really meant to say was simply this: I knew of no place where I wanted a home because I didn't know what home was.

A year after Father's death, the pined-for family vacation happens at long last. We gather in Turkey where Naveen now lives and is expecting her first child. As we march along the streets of old Istanbul, donning our hats and cameras, it feels as if we have done this many times before. We mount a ferry on the Marmara Sea, crossing over from the Asian side of Istanbul to the European side, the geographical attribute that denotes the region as Eurasia. From the deck of the ferry I stare at the famous Bosphorus Bridge connecting the two sides and I cannot help but marvel at its significance. If you stand right in the middle of the Bosphorus Bridge you stand in the centre of the space that is neither Europe nor Asia. There is great debate among geologists over the formation of the narrow channel of water that connects the edges of Europe and Asia in the body of their gracious host, modern-day Turkey. Thousands of years ago, the Black Sea disconnected from the Aegean Sea which split up the land spaces of Greece and Turkey as we know them today. In around 5600 BCE, the Bosphorus appeared as an outcome of the great Mediterranean floods, to reconnect the severed seas and therefore the severed lands by way of the Sea of Marmara (which is connected by the Dardanelles to the Aegean Sea, and thereby to the Mediterranean Sea). It was because of the Bosphorus that Constantinople was built as the capital of the Eastern Roman Empire and because of the Bosphorus that the Ottomans were able to take it over in 1453.

Governments have fought over the Bosphorus forever, because of its strategic importance, and the world wars, like all other wars before them, misused the space of her charitable body which wants nothing other than to connect.

Today, the Bosphorus Bridge is a lure of hip tourism, the means of crossing over from Europe to Asia without leaving the country. As I cross it myself, my Turkish brother-in-law points out with pride, 'Now *this* you will not find in any other country.' What boggles my mind, after spending three months in beautiful Turkey, is how the people, passionate and warm, cleanly separate their Eastern values from their Western ones, as if the Bosphorus Bridge itself is invisibly suspended in their minds.

As everyone settles into a balmy evening of barbecue on the patio of our villa, I search online for more Bosphorus-related trivia. On 15 May 2005 at 7.00 local time, US tennis star Venus Williams played a show game with Turkish standout Ipek Şenoğlu on the bridge, the first tennis match ever to be played on two continents. The event was organised as a promotion ahead of the 2005 WTA's Istanbul Cup and lasted five minutes only on the north side of the bridge. After the exhibition, both players threw a tennis ball into the Bosphorus.

The last sentence makes me think. Why throw the tennis ball into the Bosphorus? What promise of friendship did two opposing parties proclaim through this act? Was the throwing of the ball a truce, an attempt at a civil relationship, despite the results of the match? Or was it something more? A gentle wish, perhaps, for a future world where territorial demarcations will not be necessary to define ourselves.

Indeed, there is a popular belief that if you make a wish while passing under the Bosphorus Bridge it will come true.

What could have led to this myth? Could it be that the Bosphorus, bridging the gap between two remarkably different worlds, East and West, symbolises that real harmony lies in neither this nor that. Feeling at home, being at ease, achieving happiness, being fulfilled – call it what you will – is an Eternal Bosphorus that is neither here nor there but somewhere in between. Maybe the wise ones knew this; maybe they knew that the Bosphorus was the earth's own conjugal point of oneness and harmony, because it urges us to dissociate, to step on neutral ground where we can face ourselves more candidly. So when we stand upon that place or pass under it, earth and spirit blend into a synonymous whole, commanding the right to a wish.

Pondering on the meaning of home on this July evening, in an old house in Istanbul, where I am vacationing with my family on foreign soil for the first time, I have never felt more rooted, more sheltered. Would Father have liked it here? I try to picture him sitting next to my mother on the spacious ottoman as she contentedly sips her Turkish coffee. I see him engrossed in his reveries, as he always was, contemplating the foamy outline of the Mediterranean Sea in the horizon. Would his presence, right here right now, have completed his quest? Is this what he had been looking for? As the Japanese poet Basho said:

> The moon and the sun are eternal travellers. Even the years
>   wander on.
> A lifetime adrift in a boat, or in old age leading a tired horse
>   into the years,
> every day is a journey, and the journey itself is home.

Though I am intrigued by the words, illuminated by their essence, I am not convinced by them and neither would Father have been, I suspect. If the journey itself is home, why do we so avidly await its end, so that we may return to where we belong – our home?

And now, sixteen years after my father's death, I find that neither the completion nor depletion of his life matters to me. I find myself indifferent to his achievements, forgetting his shortcomings, turning away from the gloom of his last years and searching for something beyond. Who had he been, that preoccupied man, the youngest of six children, apple of his mother's eye? He was born in the foggy mountains of Sylhet; his mother was an Assamese woman to whom I bear an eerie resemblance. My father's father was a giant of a man who loved weapons and hunting. Elephant tusks, tiger skins and stuffed deer heads were strewn across the walls of my paternal grandparents' sprawling townhouse. I never saw my grandfather. Other than the animal parts, an old hunting rifle rusting in our garage was the only memento we had of him. I vaguely remember my grandmother before she died. I was just five at the time. In her white sari, she was indiscernible from the huge white bed that was slowly swallowing her up.

'Come, little one, come close so I can see,' she'd say, reaching for me with a shrivelled hand.

'No,' I would reply every time, hiding my face in my father's lap, 'I'm scared of your wrinkles.'

'Give Dadu a kiss,' my father would urge, picking me up and putting me on the bed next to my grandmother.

He must have wanted me to love his mother. He once said she was his favourite person in the world.

I pick up bits and pieces of my father from his family and friends.

'Your father was a mischief maker. He would just disappear for hours, making everyone very worried,' says my aunt, showing me a picture of a twelve-year-old boy, standing barefoot on the grass, pristine tea gardens rising behind him.

I take a closer look at the boy in the photograph. He was very lean, bony almost, and his eyes sparkled with amusement. I am trying hard to remember the times I'd seen my father amused. Why is my memory failing me?

All these details I collect about my father seem increasingly useless as the years go by. They are nothing but fragments that fail to elucidate the whole. There was the wild, daredevil boy growing up in the mountains amongst deer and tigers. Then there was the dashing young man of later years, the man who broke a lot of women's hearts before he fell in love with my mother's voice. There was also the eccentric man who protected his car as if it was alive, the elegant and ambitious man whose work consumed him completely, and finally, the faithful soul who knelt in daily prayer in search of the peace that he could not, ultimately, find in his life. But where was *my* father in all of this? Why does he come to me only as a metaphor for some ideal, like ambition or devotion or duty? Why can't I fill the ever-present distance between him and I with anything other than the longing to know more?

I am tired of remembering my father in the context of his circumstances. I am tired of the mystery and silence shadowing his very image. I wish to see him without the burden of his life, without his successes and failures and responsibilities, without his rituals and beliefs. I wish to meet him again, as I would a stranger. Sometimes when I enter a restaurant or walk down the street and I catch a glimpse of a curly head with a gaunt face, I turn sharply in the hope of receiving a further sign. A smile perhaps, a meaningful look, an absurd but familiar gesture – anything that will signal to me that my father has returned to reveal himself to me, to bridge the gap that kept widening between us when he was my father and I his daughter. In this new meeting, all that exists between us is the present moment, bubbling with the urgency to know each other.

Deep End

Lead my mother to an overflowing bathtub and she will shriek. Pretend to push her into a swimming pool and she may never speak to you again. Take her for a boat ride in the middle of a choppy ocean and she will faint from fear. My mother has severe hydrophobia and to make sure that her children were not afflicted with the same condition, she sent us for swimming lessons.

Two afternoons a week, Naveen, Tilat and I turned up for our lessons at the Dhaka Women's Sports Complex. The large, outdoor swimming pool was a courageous choice for a women's facility in Dhaka, given how our open-air frolicking was daily witnessed by varied audiences with their noses pressed against their windows. Though it upset our swimming coach, some of the older women refused the slightest exposition of skin and therefore any kind of swimsuit and instead dragged their fully clothed bodies into the pool. When they swam, their long loose tunics ballooned above and around them, making them look like freakish, menacing water creatures.

I loved the water and I learned to float and swim quickly, that is, until it was time to tackle the deep end of the pool. I swam vertically across the pool, staying close to the wall. As soon as I sensed proximity to the deep end, I bobbed my head out of the water and grabbed on to the wall, refusing to swim any further. My coach was frustrated. She assured me, repeatedly, that she would never let me drown, that she was following right behind me. But my body was more stubborn than I. Before the final act of suspending myself over a depth that I could neither feel with my feet nor assess with my eyes, I was overcome by a fear that was, perhaps, no different from my mother's.

'I am ready to give up,' announced the coach. 'What will it take for you to just let yourself go in the deep end?'

I thought about it. In order for me to let loose in deep water, a place which my cells are preconditioned to flee, I would have to forget the weight and feel of my own body, would need to disconnect from the thrumming of my heart and the buzzing of my brain. But how was that possible? And yet, how was it that I had floated, in perfect safety and serenity, in the first waters of my life, tucked inside a pear-shaped organ for nine nourishing months? How was it that in those unknown waters, survival was never a question and fear never a hindrance?

I had thought, wrongly, misguidedly, that overcoming fear was a kind of self-deprecating act. I didn't see then, as I do now, that fear doesn't always hold us back from good things, it also warns us against the bad.

And so, in the beginning, the trepidation that overcomes me at the sight and sound of Yameen makes me think that it is simply my fear of the unknown – an irrational and conquerable fear. My first conversation with him takes place by pure accident, if there is such a thing as an accident. Yameen knows my college roommate Lyn and calls one day to say hello to her. I, who have been sitting at Lyn's desk casually munching on cashew nuts and gazing at the fine spring morning, happen to pick up her phone. Yameen and I exchange polite introductions and I offer to take a message for Lyn. The same evening he calls again. This time Lyn answers and he asks for me. Both Lyn and I are puzzled. 'Do you know him?' she asks. 'Because I barely do.' I shake my head vigorously but curiosity gets the better of me. For the next five months, Yameen calls me several times every day.

I do not know why I speak to him any more than he knows why he calls but I am dimly aware of a tug, a pull. There is something manic about the nature of this pull. My conversations with Yameen are strange, dreamy and vaguely unnerving. I regard the strangeness and the discomfort as necessary parts of the beguiling whole, the *whole* being romance. After all, no one expects love to be ordinary, familiar. Associated with the 'fall' of falling in love are the promissory qualities of surprise and serendipity. We expect the interior of love to be laced with unknowns, pleasurable ones, which we will discover, bit by delicious bit.

'Why do you keep calling me?' I ask him.

'Because I want to know you.'

'Why?'

'I don't know.'

'That's not a convincing answer.'

'I feel that we have a connection.'

'We haven't even met.'

'I know. I cannot explain it. Can you always explain every-thing you feel?'

I am fascinated by the way he implicates the two of us in a budding relationship based on one fated call. What is romance, if it doesn't leave us open-mouthed, wondering from where it came or how then to proceed? Think of the sudden gust of wind romancing through a peacefully sunny day, lifting the hats and newspapers off unsuspecting heads and hands. Think, too, of the unfathomable romance between the poet Rumi and his Beloved, the Beloved he never saw, except in his own heart.

Is it possible that the persuasion of Yameen's words lie not in their construction but my conception of them? Because, in later years, no matter how much I will try, I will not find a trace of the old vigour and furor in him. Do I attribute these qualities to our conversations out of my own need for them? Has he become for me Rumi's God, the Divine Lover, who can do no wrong, whose cruelty is a cause for rejoicing? I check out four volumes of Rumi's poetry from the library and pore over them. When I find what I am looking for, I type them in bold and pin them above my desk:

> Oh friend, seek no joy when the Beauty desires
> heartache, for you are prey in a lion's claws.
> Should the Heart-ravisher pour mud on your
> Head, welcome it in place of Tartarian musk.

But am I willing to surrender or am I looking to devour? The tug I feel is of this deep and ancient hunger. I have felt the plunder of this hunger before, rolling on the floor of my room during long days of fasting. It told me then as it tells me now of its insatiable nature. I am the true Heart-ravisher. I look to ravish my own heart and then some, so large is my appetite for this Thing. The Thing. Is it romance? It is more than that. It is satiety itself, a kind of jigsaw-puzzle wholesomeness when all the pieces are aligned. It requires divination because nothing will ever present itself in perfect form. I will make my lover divine through voracious devotion. Eager to spur this sublimation, I let Yameen convince me of the inevitability of our match. I let him speak of our union as a matter of time not chance. Smart as a whip, he guesses my bait and reels me in, slowly, salaciously.

'If I can want you so much without seeing you, imagine how much I will want you when we are together,' he whispers.

'You could be disappointed too,' I say.

'Not a chance.'

'You never know.'

'One always knows – if only one allows oneself to see.'

'And you see what?'

'In you, I see everything.'

His words, whether premeditated or chosen carefully on the spur of the moment, hurtle through me, bullet-like, past the years, and detonate my truest desire. The desire to be seen, to be heard, to shed my invisibility and abandon my hiding places. No wonder my wish to believe him is far stronger than his wish to be believed.

Is it a surprise then that on our first date, I am disappointed to see Yameen in the flesh? By this I do not mean the way he looks but the fact that he has a body, with a specific shape and size. A body, that circumscribes his limitations and contains his impact. To me, he has been the limitless, amorphous voice who speaks to me about love. His voice has been my guiding light to The Thing. To see him standing before me, so human, so measurable and distinct, so bound by dimensions, is to admit the death of a magical voice that alone can promise magical things.

He takes me to the top of the World Trade Center where we sip grass-green mojitos and look down at the sleepless city twinkling below. Awkwardness blots the air between us. What now? Are we to continue our fantasy discussions or dance the night away? We find a way to mask our unshakeable discomfiture. We drag ourselves from bar to bar as if it is our sole mission for the night. I am not sure how much time passes before we end up at a bar called Odeon in Tribeca, with a big blue neon sign outside. I am starting to feel ill.

'No more bars,' I say out loud, the first one of us to succumb to reality.

'We must end the night with a cosmo,' he says. 'It's a New York thing.'

I end up having seven.

Why has he never mentioned before his wild years as a student at Columbia and afterwards in his hip, L-shaped apartment on the Upper West Side?

'It was easy to pick up both cocaine and women back then,' he says, not noticing my faint frown. He explains what it means to be an old-school roller skater on Sunday afternoons in Central Park. 'Kids these days don't know how to roller skate. They just try to look cool,' he sniggers and then sighs. 'New York has changed so much. You can't even buy weed at the corner of 116th and Amsterdam any more.'

I am not alert enough to ponder why a twenty-nine-year-old reminisces about a New York from before his time. I do not wonder why he looks so sober after three hours of non-stop drinking. Instead, I allow myself to drown in the memories of our impassioned telephone musings on love and commitment. I see now how desperate I was to love what seemed impossible to love. It proved some kind of unmatchable victory to me that made little sense in the context of normal victories. But back then, I believed what I had been taught – that life was a test, a mountain, and the steeper the climb the better the view on top.

I glance up at the illusive Manhattan sky before getting into the back of a yellow cab with Yameen, feeling sick to the stomach. Is there a low moon floating behind one of the skyscrapers or am I hallucinating?

He is asking me a lot of questions. I nod and nod, hoping to stop the torrent of questions. Where are those ever-convincing whispers now, lilting lullabies across the miles between our phones?

'Are you sure?' I hear him say. He looks uneasy. I am about to tell him that I have no idea what he is talking about, that I am sure of nothing at the moment, but my chest heaves, an avalanche of bitterness floods my gullet and I lose consciousness.

The next morning when I wake up on an old mattress on the floor of a dank Jersey City room, my first instinct is distrust. All around me are signs of decay: filthy, misshapen blinds on the windows, the painting of a woman hanging crookedly on the wall and gathering dust, a chipped nightstand with no handle. The floors are strewn with junk mail and dirty laundry. In one corner of the room, cardboard boxes are stacked as if no one has ever found the time to open them. In the insalubrious interior of this home, if it can be called a home, my resolve for romance begins to disintegrate. I gather up my things and scramble down the stairwell, hoping not to run into the man from the night before. But I find him outside, sitting in the shade with a beer in his hand, two empty bottles at his feet. 'Wait,' he says disquietingly, 'you're not leaving just yet.'

Being with Yameen makes me feel heavy, as if I am wading through water with stones tied to my ankles. The rapture of the phone conversations is long lost, scraped clean from the bond we attempt to recreate with our flesh. The effect he administers on me, since our meeting in New York, is that of a sedative. As if I am a person who needs to be put to sleep, he obliterates all activity from my life. He hardly lets me visit him in New York any more. Every weekend he rents a car and drives up to my college to see me. If we leave my room at all to smoke joints and eat cheap Chinese take-out, it is because we run out of food or my stash of candy bars and potato chips. Other than Lyn, who already knows him, he refuses to meet anyone else. He does not let me give him a tour of my campus, nor does he accompany me to the little cafe where I like to sit and read. He tells me he is not interested in my dance performances.

The commonalities in our backgrounds do not bring us any closer. Yameen was born to Tanzanian parents who moved to America when he was a child. He too, was born into a Muslim family. Later I find that his family is large like mine, as well as loud and chaotic. The only difference is, Yameen stands outside of their chaos. He withdraws from them, as he withdraws from me, and as he teaches me to withdraw from everyone else.

But if Yameen sedates me, if he hoists my unconscious weight on his shoulders and carries me to isolation, it is only because I do not kick and flail during my undoing. The teetering isolation I had imposed on myself through dancing and by forsaking music is simply solidified by the segregation that Yameen commands. I let him do it, finding twisted comfort in renouncing a world I am already barred from – the world of music. The soporific lull of our strange relationship only wears off if I mistakenly try to reach out to him. His eyes blaze with malice if I ask him about his family, his friends or his past, stopping me in mid-sentence. If I tell him about my own family he indiscreetly turns the other way. Foolishly, I let myself find comfort in this too. Maybe I am enough for him, I reason. Maybe all he cares about is *me*, outside of the context of my roots, my past, my future. But how can I think this possible? What dislocation of body and spirit has allowed me to feel that I exist without the impact of my birth and history?

I am pleasantly surprised to find Yameen's parents' home unlike his own. It is a well-tended house, well-loved and lived in. A beautiful Japanese maple tree stands up tall in the front-yard, partially blocking the rectangular New England-style cottage, made modern with sparkling glass doors and windows. I walk through the rooms one by one, inhaling the dry sweet scents of potpourri and orange deodoriser. There are two small, sunny rooms adjacent to each other that used to belong to his sisters. The bed frames look fragile but the bedspreads have bright blue and pink patchwork quilts and the window-sills and dressers are covered with old dolls and stuffed animals that have no doubt been kept clean over the years. There are old photographs of his sisters laughing and playing on the beach, posing in prom dresses, as well as pictures of their children as newborns and toddlers. There is another slightly bigger room that had belonged to Yameen's brother. The walls here are covered with pictures of high school and college football teams, trophies and other football knick-knacks. This room too is scrubbed clean and bathed in sunlight.

The large living room shows similar signs of care. The furniture is old but classic. The silk upholstery has a delicate blue and white floral print that is fading but the wood has been polished to a noticeable brilliance. More family pictures are displayed in colour-coordinated frames and an elaborate flower arrangement rests in the middle of the coffee table. A heavy crystal chandelier hangs directly above it. I am getting anxious to see Yameen's room.

After mentioning it several times, Yameen leads me to his room with reluctance. We go down to the basement, walk through a laundry and storage space and stop in front of a small dark room. A narrow bed is covered with a ragged-looking brown quilt; next to it stands an old battered dresser. A half torn poster of Pelé is plastered to the dirty wall and several pairs of old sneakers are lined up against some storage boxes on the opposite wall. This room resembles the Jersey City room; it has the same aura of pure desolation. Why has he been given this dungeon of a room in this big, handsome house? Is this where he spent all his time, like an unwelcome guest, cut off from the rest of the family? He reads my mind.

'My father thought it was best for me to have more privacy.'

'Why?' I ask.

He shrugs.

'Let's go,' I say, taking his hand. 'It's too dark in here.'

Yameen's words leave me with a portentous chill. Something in the way he says 'my father' invokes loss, too great to acknowledge. So I let it go as I try to shush the little voice in my head telling me never to return to that house.

I do not know where my first year with Yameen rolls away, bringing me close to my college graduation day. It had been the most consequential and yet the most listless year of my life. I receive in my mailbox a sheaf of envelopes that reflect my academic achievements but I feel hollow, uninformed and unprepared for anything outside the classroom. Mother comes to attend my graduation and I agonise over the prospect of her meeting Yameen. With characteristic directness, she observes, shortly after her first encounter with him, 'He is twenty-nine years old, you say?'

'Yes, why?'

'Because he isn't.'

'Mother!'

'Trust me, he is not twenty-nine. Have you seen his passport or driver's licence?'

'No, of course not.'

'Then you should.'

I decide not to contradict her, not now, when I stand on the brink of a new chapter in my new world with my new lover. The old world is far behind and what Mother says sounds bizarre enough to ignore. Besides, both my mother and I are so much better at leaving things unsaid. Mother is polite to Yameen. She smiles and speaks in her usual charming manner. I see through her act, I see the suspicion skulking under her smile, and I prepare myself for further accusations. I am still at the bottom of a cavernous sleep, my subconscious waiting for an alarm clock to jolt me out of its numbing depths. But she never brings it up again. More surprisingly, she sleeps arduously through the entire trip. All day long she sleeps, waking up for dinner, before retiring early. I jot it down to jetlag, trying to overlook that, unlike jetlaggers, she never wakes at improbable hours. Around Yameen her eyes shine with distrust though her lips remain sealed. She had already spoken and I had not listened.

After graduation weekend, the three of us drive back to New York together. As soon as we're there Mother stops sleeping all day, as if a curse has been lifted off her. We shop, eat out, visit parks and museums. We pretend that she never met Yameen until I decide she should meet his parents. My proposition makes Yameen unhappy and Mother uncomfortable but they both agree, albeit grudgingly. His parents extend an invitation for lunch.

On a gorgeous Saturday afternoon, the three of us meet near Grand Central Station to catch a train to Scarsdale. Yameen offers to show my mother around the area. We walk past the famous Chrysler building and buy coffee and smoked almonds from a vendor. My mother, an infatuated shopper, wanders into every store in sight. An hour passes. Yameen seems in no hurry to head back to the station.

'Why don't we walk to Bryant Park and show her Fifth Avenue on the way?' he suggests.

'What about your parents? We don't want to be late for lunch,' says Mother.

'Don't worry, they wake up late on Saturdays. They asked us to take our time.'

'Are you sure?'

'Positive.'

We kill another hour before making our way to the train station. The shades are drawn in the living room of his parents' home although it's only two in the afternoon when we arrive. The house is horribly quiet. Mother and I sit uneasily in the living room while Yameen disappears inside.

'You've met them before?' Mother enquires.

'Yes, once.' I do not tell her about the appalling sight of Yameen's dingy basement room.

When Yameen's parents arrive, it is obvious they have just been woken. They look dishevelled and yawn as they shake our hands. His mother offers to put some water on for tea and arranges a plate of crackers. The five of us exchange awkward tidbits about the weather and sports. How much time passes? It is hard to tell with the heavy drapes blocking daylight. Even after several cups of tea and many cumbersome pauses in the conversation, no one mentions lunch. I have no choice but to take Yameen aside and demand an explanation.

'I thought this was a lunch invitation?'

'So did I.'

'Did they actually invite us or did you make it up?'

'I think they did . . .'

'You *think*?'

'It wasn't supposed to be formal.'

'There is *no* lunch, formal *or* informal.'

I know Yameen will not confront his parents. Had I known, too, the unavoidable haplessness of such a meeting? How can I blame this man before me when I can so well understand the physics of his self-effacement?

Yameen ambles back to the living room and cheerfully announces that he is going to order some food from the local Indian restaurant. His parents immediately say they are not hungry.

'We usually don't eat lunch on Saturdays, we just have an early dinner,' says his mother, unfazed and detached.

I fix my eyes on the red and green carpet, not daring to meet my mother's questioning ones. When the delivery man brings our food, we eat, only because eating eases the onus of talking and looking at each other. We have run out of things to say about the weather and Yameen's father is now fixated on the sports channel, blocking everyone else from his vision. Their relief, when we get up to leave, is painfully conspicuous. On the way back from Scarsdale, no one utters a word. My mother sleeps through the entire train ride.

The day my mother leaves, I accompany her to the airport. We both know I am going to move in with Yameen after her departure. She does not dare say what I dare not ask. We sip cappuccinos at the airport Starbucks, the air between us as it always is – an unsung song.

A year later, I find Yameen's passport discreetly hidden under a pile of old papers, shoved to the back of his closet, next to an empty bottle of tequila. He is seven years older than he claims to be, which would have made him thirty-six at the time he said he was twenty-nine. I had been waiting for a grand rescue, for my mother to declare her sweeping objections to my lover that would open my eyes and end my anguish. But she had, in the most ineffective of ways, given me an effective clue. Neither of us had ever been able to let ourselves go at the deep end of things. We were accustomed to passing our days in a comradeship of forced peacefulness. So, also when it came to love, we could not look each other in the eye. I was fifteen, when Mother had discovered a boy under my bed. It was not so much the terrified youngster under the bed as the sight of the rumpled bed sheets that sent her into a fit of rage and she told me that the foulness of my choices would continue to haunt me as a woman.

'You disgusting little creature – to give your body to a boy at your age! What will you have left to give to a man by the time you are a woman?'

Was she hesitant now to chastise me with the same conviction because I was older or because she had already made her prediction years ago? Still, as Mother walked away from me at the airport, pulling her worn suitcase along, her pace noticeably slow and tired, a part of me sensed her defeat.

'You fell in love with my music,' she always used to say to my father. Did she really mean to say that he had never fallen in love with her?

We both thrashed about in shallow waters, my mother and I, while the truth sank to the bottom.

The view from the window hardly ever changes. Young Puerto Ricans and elderly Indians hoist their overloaded laundry bags across littered sidewalks. A few androgynous looking teenagers dressed in oversized T-shirts and denims saunter by, callously flinging their cigarette butts and crumpled soda cans on the street. The paraplegic old man next door sits on his porch, staring dismally ahead. The little Russian lady, a dirty blue scarf knotted under her chin, tip-toes up to my herb garden and starts ripping out bunches of coriander, oregano and basil. This is my neighbourhood in Jersey City, a place whose spirit bears no buoyancy. This is a place of cheerless cohabitation, a mangled place, licking its wounds and regarding the rest of the world through suspicious eyes. Like Yameen.

By eight in the morning, I run out of my apartment to catch a bus into Manhattan. The bus I am on is not really a bus. It is half the size of a regular bus, carrying less than twenty people and driven by unlicenced Puerto Ricans and Dominicans. They drive at the speed of light and the passengers are expected to sacrifice their safety for the lowered fare they pay. I see an aisle seat and race for it, hoping to stay away from the window seats to avoid rubbing up against the grimy, sweaty vinyl interior of the van. My triumph is short-lived. As I settle into my seat, a huge woman lumbers into the van and comes straight towards me.

'Move,' she growls, without looking up from the message she is typing on her phone.

I scoot over to the window. I am burning up in my winter coat but there is no room now to stretch my arms and take off my coat. I don't want to antagonise this hostile woman in her oversized fake fur coat, clutching a paperback between bright red nail extensions, a glossy, pink phone studded with shiny rhinestones, dangling from her wrist.

Forty minutes later, I am standing in front of the coffee vendor. I buy my usual large Colombian coffee with extra sugar and two glazed donuts. I justify the decadent breakfast by reminding myself of the bundle of energy I will need to get through the day. By the time I make it to the forty-fifth floor of the shining black high-rise in the middle of 6th Avenue, I am already beat.

My boss Jess, who is five years older than me, pops her head into my cubicle and snorts at my donuts. She has dropped me enough hints about good gyms in the area where I can take advantage of our corporate discount policy. Jess is tall, thin, blond and vastly irritating. My co-workers call her 'The Clit', presumably (I never confirmed) meaning she resembles a clitoris. I also never know which they mean to insult more, Jess or the female labia. This morning, Jess wants to sell me her blue couch because she is moving into her fiancé's apartment in Jersey City. I don't want her couch, or anything else that has come into intimate contact with her flat bottom, but it gives me considerable pleasure to think that she is giving up her life in Manhattan to live in the tri-state area's most depressing corner.

I never thought I would live in Jersey City until Yameen convinced me to move in with him. After college, I had planned to move to New York and live in Manhattan. Manhattan is said to have something for everyone but my relationship with it is sensate. In this city, I am acutely aware of standing at the breathless, gaping mouth of a giant organism which inhales, drawing me into the conundrum of its insides and then exhales, spitting me out. I am especially baffled by how the city morphs between the hours of light and darkness. When the morning sun glints off the glass panes of the high rises, turning everything into a smouldering gold, I love standing way below to look up and see that ethereal glow sweeping the expanse of the city. Just then, Manhattan feels silken, serene, tranquil. But after dark, she becomes a criss-cross of secretive alleyways and back-streets, each with their own sass and savour: smoky jazz bars uptown, breezy Soho terraces, the blue-black and purple velvet of East Village haunts, the ersatz lounges of the meat-packing district, the lamp-lit windows of the elegant Fifth Avenue townhouses, and in each of these places, the sovereign quality is mystery. This mystery plagues me as I stand by my kitchen window in Jersey City from where I can just about catch a glimpse of the Empire State Building. Steeped in the stifling darkness of my surroundings, I think of men and women, delicate glasses in their hands, clinking them together late into a mystifying night. I strain to hear their laughter, their conversations. And I feel the pulse of that other world beating with the romance that is lacking in mine. I wonder at the nature of my life for it was not so long ago when I had fled from Dhaka, allured by the auspices of America. Now, here in America, I am no more grounded than I was, no closer to home. Once again, I find myself drifting between realities, unfastened from the one I am in, alien to the one I covet.

Jess pops her head back into my cubicle around 5.30 p.m. to say goodbye and, as soon as she leaves, I turn off my computer and walk out into the biting winter evening. I decide to walk through the theatre district. I enjoy watching throngs of excited tourists crowding into the local bars to get a little tipsy before going to their favourite Broadway shows. I stop under the half-nude Calvin Klein model in Times Square and watch the street performers move to their funky beats. They bring soul to the plastic flesh of Times Square.

Soon, too soon, I am waiting for my bus back to Jersey. When I get off at Thorne Street, I walk down the dark sidewalk, praying that this terrible, frosty loneliness is just a figment of my imagination. I pray that when I walk in through the door and step into the cracked, crippled apartment I call home, I will not notice the shabbiness, but instead, will run straight into the arms of the man I claim to love. This never happens. I always smell the stale furniture and note the peeling linoleum kitchen floor. I know the reason I notice these things. It is because I try not to notice the man I live with. Every day I think of what it would be like to turn the clock back to two years ago. Like my mother, I too dream of unstitching the seam of my story. Just like Mother, I keep staring at life, wondering when it will gratify me.

'We cannot sponsor you for a work visa,' says Jim, the head of the equities department. 'You have a degree in Philosophy and Religion. How will that justify your work as an insurance broker?'

I usually like Jim's no-nonsense straightforwardness, but this time I balk at his words before reminding him that I had been hired based on those very qualifications, thought to be 'well rounded' and 'diverse' at the time. I had also done fine work for almost a year, with whatever knowledge my degree had proffered on me.

'Jim!' I say, accusingly. 'This means I may have to return to Bangladesh. Without my work permit I cannot stay and there is no time to find something else.'

'You have a few months before you have to leave ...' Jim tells me, calmly.

The problem, however, isn't Jim. It is Immigration and Naturalisation Services. I stare at Jim's clean-shaven, square-ish Korean face. What he proclaims about the company's inability to draw a credible connection between my work and my education may be true but someone must have known that at the time I was hired. I want to ask him about Beth from Iowa, also a Religion major, who sits in the cubicle next to mine. She has worked for the company for five years and is about to be promoted. Then there are the Art History and English majors from Long Island and Alabama, whose jobs do not seem to be on the line.

So why, I ask Jim, did the company hire me in the first place? Am I simply an error in their massive chain of operations? Is my name a small number that doesn't add up and needs simply to be deleted from the balance sheet before the new fiscal year starts? The interview, hardly a year old, is still fresh on my mind.

'I can adapt to new environments well,' I had said with great confidence. 'You see, I've lived away from home for four years and have had to adjust to many changes.'

Pens clicked furiously; heads bobbed up and down in sympathy.

'I grew up in South Africa. I know how hard it is to start a new life in a new country,' said a thin girl with brown hair.

Everyone sat back and let me impress them with promises of some exotic strength, the strength to forsake and build anew, to start over. A strength I seem to be lacking at the thought of returning to Dhaka. Why is it I feel unhinged at the thought of returning to the home of my childhood? After all, I don't even like my work. Deep inside, I am grateful to be released from the morose routine of my life. But what am I to do in Dhaka? The question poses an insurmountable void, a black hole of uncertainty.

'What are you so afraid of?' Yameen asks. 'You're only going home.'

Home. The home I left behind five years ago has changed. My father is dead, Naveen has married and moved to a different country, Tilat has married and moved to a different house, my mother has finally immersed herself in music the way she had always dreamed of doing, and sweet, spirited Avi has turned into a reclusive young man I hardly recognise. Without all the members of my family under one roof, without the old kinesthesia of our beings against each other, I cannot decode the vision of my home, abounding in its sights, sounds and smells. The body of my home is the conflation of six bodies, those bodies now scattered across the continents, consumed by their ownness, in this life or another. I cannot gravitate upon the surface of such a barren and unfamiliar home. I float above it, like an aircraft caught in a blinding storm, hovering over safety but unable to get to it.

'We should start thinking about marriage,' I say to Yameen, as I start the preparations to return to Dhaka. The words fall off my mouth like reckless mountain jumpers willing to risk any peril in the name of their obsession.

'Really?' Yameen sounds incredulous.

'Yes, really.'

'You're sure?'

Sureness is no longer a reasonable expectation.

I marry Yameen more than two years after we first meet and only six months after I leave New York and return to Dhaka. The decision is made after a long bout of squabbling and bickering with each other. Every single time we fight we buy a cheap bottle of vodka, drink ourselves silly and broach the subject of marriage. Instead of bidding each other the goodbyes that are long overdue, we hold on to each other in fierce desperation. We are two valiant soldiers, weary from battle but determined not to lay down our arms.

When I get to Dhaka, I confide in some friends about my apathy for my husband-to-be and my doubts about the imminent wedding. They laugh and pat me on the back and tell me that married life will be wonderful. Having been away for five years, I cannot discern the thin line between politeness and sincerity. My mother, now inside the solid armour of her life, finds her voice. With the confidence of a queen she declares that all marriages are bland. It is up to the woman to choose the flavour she adds to it.

But the talons of despair dig deeper and deeper into me and I find myself waking up earlier and earlier in the mornings, long before the sun appears and the day disappears into yet another chasm of wedding planning. These pre-dawn moments are all I have to myself. I huddle in one corner of the little balcony among the overgrown basil and mint plants and stay there until I hear my mother and Amol calling me to breakfast.

I met Jeetu during those bewildering days, when I lived every moment in the eye of a storm. He thundered into my life with the speed of lightning from the moment we met at a friend's backyard barbeque. Jeetu's longish hair, loose white shirts and inexhaustible appetite for all things prohibited often reminded me of the young Jim Morrison whose music he so loved. He turned up at our doorstep one evening, muttering something incomprehensive, sweating profusely, his white shirt covered in pink lipstick stains. I held his hand

and led him to the roof, placed him in one of the green plastic chairs and gave him a glass of cold water. Almost every night since then, we sat together on those hideous green chairs, late into the night, tied in a kind of doomed solidarity. If Jeetu's wife ever questioned where he was, I presumed he never answered her truthfully. For although Jeetu and I were friends of a kind at heart, both our bodies were trained for forbidden pleasure. We kissed and petted and fondled each other without much thought. It was mostly a way of making sure that we were still alive and breathing despite the chill in our souls. Sometimes, when Jeetu softly hummed the notes of 'Light My Fire' or 'Riders on the Storm', I wondered, fleetingly, if I could ever fall in love with him or he with me.

The more time Jeetu and I spent together, the less we comforted each other. He told me he had married the woman he loved and I told him that I was about to marry a man I didn't love. But I didn't understand his distress and indiscretions any more than he understood my self-inflicting pain. He proclaimed a passion for living that was continually betrayed by his destructive lifestyle. I waved my life away with casual abandon yet tried desperately to inject it with clarity. Jeetu had no interest in my books, in travel or philosophy or history; he filled his cup with his own muddled existence and was perplexed, every day, at how much there was to consider. My need to tear an idea to bits, to chew on words and belabour my thoughts was lost on him.

We sat facing each other across the luminous night sky, wishing we could help each other. Sometimes we went for aimless drives along the city's deserted outskirts, Jim Morrison blasting through the stereos, the wind whipping our faces red.

Sometimes I accompanied Jeetu to an empty apartment that he kept as a music pad and he beat wildly against a drum set while I sat in a barely furnished room with a bunch of strangers and drank vodka from a paper cup. We never had long discussions or arguments or even much small talk between us. We knew the important details of each other's lives but left the rest to chance. We simply sought to be in each other's presence all the time and were both astonished at how our hearts stopped racing as soon as we were within a few feet of each other. He was my magic potion and I his.

Jeetu and I should have kept our doomed solidarity intact, within those puzzling, clandestine, rooftop meetings. Where there is odd chemistry and inexplicable charisma, sex itself is often not as satisfying as its anticipation.

I was bright with excitement when Jeetu arrived one evening. Something in the way he moved and talked told me it was going to be different that night. My sisters had invited all our cousins to help them paint the invitation cards for my Holud, the Bengali equivalent of a hen party. Jeetu peered over their shoulders and said something that made them all laugh. I stood in the doorway watching his silhouette; he turned and smiled and I knew what he wanted but I didn't know it was the last time he would smile at me like that.

In his own way Jeetu was trying to be kind to me that night. We sped through the city streets and up the three flights of stairs to his empty music pad until we stood, breathless and naked, before each other. And then we were stuck, prey to the quicksand of our sudden vacillation. I covered my body with my bare arms and turned away. He pulled me into his arms, stroked my cheeks and gently reminded me that I must start married life without guilt. I was touched by his tenderness but the fact that we never made love despite our deep kisses and warm caresses left me suddenly clairvoyant. Jeetu, dear friend and antidote to my gloom, could no more save me from myself than Mother or Father or anyone else. He withdrew his magic at the cusp of salvation. If only he had allowed me to feel that what was forbidden could also be unforbidden, with just a touch, a look, a whisper. If only he had allowed himself to see that neither love nor its absence was something to be ashamed of.

A month before my wedding, I have a dream. I see my wedding party taking place on an unusually warm January afternoon. All the guests perspire in their winter attire and one old man suffers a heat stroke. We move to the garden in the hope of a cool breeze but the sun beats down, hot and bright. Everyone is given a cool glass of lemon water but soon the liquid dries up in our glasses. The rivers, streams and ponds begin to dry up. Pleading eyes turn to the sky to pray for rain but the sky has dried up too.

I bolt upright in bed, dizzy, feverish. I have to remind myself that I am in Dhaka, where my wedding preparations are underway. I call Yameen.

'Please, we have to call off this wedding,' I say, without preamble.

I brace myself for silence, shock, rebellion, confusion or even plain disbelief. Anything but the reaction I elicit. I hear a whining sound, starting low, then gaining momentum and turning into a demented yowl. He cries, every day, until my doubts give way to delirium. In the end, it is not that he cries or forces or begs. The loneliness we have shared and his subsequent misery at losing our inchoate bond, leads me to consent that our separation is not possible without the final despairing consummation, which is to be our marriage.

On the morning of the wedding the sky is sapphire smoke and there is a citrus fragrance in the air. I am soaped, scrubbed, bathed, brushed, powdered, blood-coloured wrapped in sheaths of chiffon and held in place by jewelled chains of gold. There is music everywhere, flowers and sweets and precocious little girls with glitter on their cheeks. I sit alone. I cannot feel my body, I am jumping off the deep end. No one pays attention to me. Any moment I expect to disperse into nothingness, leaving behind a jumble of red and gold, a cornucopia of glass, metal and fabric. By the time they place a long rectangular yard of shiny material above my head and walk me to the bridal stage, I am gone. What they see is the illusion of me, the way you see the light of a star thousands of years after it has died.

I sit on the stage and smile blankly at everyone below. At the other end of the long room, looking straight at me, stands Jeetu. His brown eyes are full of nostalgia. I close my eyes and seal an image of him in my memory – a gentle face pressed against mine, lips curled in inconsummate longing, the everlasting moment before love.

We are gathered in the kitchen of the Scarsdale house. I watch my husband finish his second bottle of wine and pop the cork of a third. His lips are a lush purple, his fingers tremble near the smudged rim of his glass. His father insists that we spend the night. I start to protest but realise that Yameen is in no condition to drive home. Both his parents retire early and Yameen falls asleep holding an empty wine bottle to his lips like a baby peacefully sucking on the nipple. I step outside into the late spring night. A half-moon laughs sideways across a star-spangled sky. I think of sleeping on the cool, moist grass, under the stars, away from the desolate house, completely unaware of the pair of eyes watching me, willing me to go back inside.

By the time I return, the house is completely dark. Someone has even switched off the light in the hallway. I have no wish to see Yameen's drunk, lifeless form in the living room where I'd left him so I turn towards the guestroom. I fumble along the walls for the light switch, my hands bumping against picture frames and coat racks. I shuffle clumsily along, freezing, as my fingers touch warm human skin.

He stands flattened against the wall. I can only make out his silhouette but I recognise his strong whisky breath.

'I thought I heard someone,' Yameen's father says calmly.

'Yameen is in the living room,' I say.

'He drinks a lot, doesn't he?' whispers his father.

'I guess so,' I'm trying to sound nonchalant.

'Every day?'

'Every day.'

'That's no good.'

I do not answer.

'Come here, let Baba give you a hug.'

'Baba,' I say, 'I'm tired. I'll see you in the morning.'

I have various fantasies, one in which Baba actually gives me a fatherly hug, another in which I move away from him in time, and yet another when Yameen's mother arrives on the scene and switches on the light, thus saving me. In reality, Baba leaps nimbly forward, wraps his huge arms around me and forces his mouth over mine. He manouevres his tongue into my mouth, swirling it around rapidly. With his arms, he holds mine down. I try to curl my own tongue in withdrawal and move my face sideways but he is too strong and too close.

The struggle goes out of me. My limbs turn flaccid. Only my voice comes out in a whimper, a muffled sound that collides threateningly into the hollow darkness. My torturer looks at me for a split second before slithering away like a creature of the night, unable to ensnare his prey. He disappears as suddenly as he had appeared.

I never mention it to Yameen. I cannot. What am I afraid of? That it will destroy our sham of a marriage? That he, the very concealer of all truth, will deny me my credibility? In truth, I am afraid that he will hear only the sound of his own heart fracturing, not mine.

One morning I wake up on the mattress on the floor of the Jersey City bedroom and a burning smell hits me. Yameen is sleeping next to me. Is there an intruder in the kitchen? A fire? An electrical short circuit? Did I leave the stove or the iron on all night? I sit up in bed with a jerk. Groggily, I try to contemplate the potential danger of the moment. I remember Yameen dismembering the smoke alarm when we lit joints the weekend before. I think of waking him but a colossal wave of sleep washes over me. I cannot fight this sleep, this heavy, cloying, numbing sleep. Weakly, I lie back on the pillow again. Is there an incandescent purple glow in the air? Do I really smell something stronger than scorched skin? I must wake up, I command myself, just before falling into a bottomless sleep.

I dream of a sea of flames, the sea bed ablaze with red-hot coals. I stand at the edge of the sea as the ends of my long hair catch fire and begin to burn. Someone is pushing me forward. I stand firm, planting my feet into the earth, trying to grip the hot, wet sand with my toes. But I cannot endure the final push. I stumble forward and feel a searing pain cut through my side. Opening my eyes, I stare into Yameen's round face above mine.

'Are you out of your mind?' he cries. 'You left the gas on all night. We could have died.'

My head reels. Shall I tell him that I had smelled the smoke and gone back to sleep? Does he think that I tried to kill us? I would never do that, would I?

I say nothing. We turn away from each other.

At about 11 a.m. on 12 September 2001, more than six months into our marriage, Yameen and I walk out of our apartment to go to the grocery store around the corner. The Jersey sky is dangerously hidden behind a thick suit of black smoke. Like all the others on the street, we walk in horrible silence, our heads bowed. Everyone is grieving and each hideous moment expands with the accretion of a collective sorrow. We are almost at the end of our block when a woman stops directly in front of us. She is a tall, stocky white woman with a shock of brown hair. She moves towards me with purposeful strides, stops less than two feet away, looks straight at me and speaks out loud.

'Go back to where you came from, you filthy foreigner. You don't belong here.'

It is the first time anyone has said anything like this to me. I am shocked, of course, partly by the lack of outrage I had expected to feel if so heinously attacked. I know the woman's words are not original; it has certainly passed through the minds of others since the planes hit the World Trade Center and for centuries before that. Still, I would have thought that when the time came for some misguided soul to unleash their hatred on me I'd leap at the great injustice of it. I would retaliate and stand up for myself and show them how wrong they were.

But all I feel is an initial jolt of surprise followed by embarrassment.

Yameen grabs my hand. 'Just keep walking. She's a nutjob.'

The woman does not look at Yameen, not even when he starts to pull me away. She stands before me, a ghastly figure, her unkempt hair lifted by the wind, pale skin, eyes narrowed in spite. Every breath she takes, each minute movement of her body is willing me to crack or bend or break. It is exactly in this instant that I feel alive again. The air comes rushing back into my lungs as if I – the drowned – have been resuscitated. My skin, dry and neglected, tingles under the midday sun. I inhale deeply the stale, forgotten odour of Jersey City. That woman, that crazy, angry God-sent woman was so very right. I didn't belong there, on the dirty sidewalk in front of a Shop Rite in Jersey City, holding Yameen's hand. I didn't belong there at all.

The woman's words – regardless of their worth – corners me into a stupefying concession of what has always eluded me – that I am living and unbroken, that even if I don't, other people can see me as I am: whole, indivisible, breathing, and tangible. The woman's castigation rips off my scabs and reveals fully the hollowness of my marriage, the concavity of my life, my attempt to be formless. By pointing her finger at me to banish me from her world, she shows me how I have been executing my own exile.

But I cannot leave my marriage, not before I chance within its confines a sudden clearing, lucid, unrestricted, brimming with possibility. I first meet Alan in the Hamptons. He is an old friend of Yameen's. He extends one long arm for a handshake while wrapping the other around a petite dark-haired girl. His red hair reminds me of a New England fall. Alan is the perfect host. He never sleeps, has his warm blue eyes on all of his guests and still manages to keep one arm around the girl. In the evenings he grills lobsters and burgers on the porch under the Amagansett sky while we drink beer and watch the stars come out.

I have never understood the ease with which some people invoke pleasure. What I knew to be pleasure always came at a cost. You had to work for it. You had to earn it. And you hardly ever deserved it. Alan, it seemed, derived genuine pleasure from the most unexpected places. He was peculiarly fond of listening to my accounts of my childhood. Voraciously, he absorbed my descriptions of the Dhaka streets, the havoc, the monsoons, the uncompromising heat. Somehow he found humour in all my misadventures; he lightened my misgivings with a broad grin, making me stop in mid-sentence, whatever sonorous tale I happened to be telling him. He felt that he knew my mother, wished that he had met my father and asked me again and again about my brother and sisters. He folded himself into the images of my past as if he had always been there in the backdrop, unnoticed but nearby. He drifted into my present, as light as a feather, lifted by a soft summer breeze.

Perhaps he saw me as I was – a memento of my past, a shadow of my present.

By our third visit to Amagansett, Alan's dark-haired friend was no longer there. 'Where is your girlfriend?' I asked, coyly.

'Who, Cynthia? Oh I've known her a long time. She likes me but she isn't my girlfriend,' he said.

I caught the hint of a smile as he assuaged my suspicion and I warned myself to be more careful. But I was hapless before Alan; I lost all design and direction. We found ourselves lying on the grass, holding hands, walking along the beach. Our attraction to each other was neither sedating nor scintillating. It was a leisurely, weightless fall into a constant state of discovery. I followed him from room to room, as he lit candle after white candle for each room of the cottage in preparation for the evening's activities. I was reminded, inadvertently, of the fragrant, candle-lit room that Father had once prepared for his wedding night but never got to see. I helped Alan clean up the empty bottles and cans and overflowing ashtrays long after all the guests had left and even in those ghostly hours of being alone together, we never kissed, never held each other close.

By the end of my first summer in Amagansett, I felt a distinct change in me. I woke up one morning on the mattress in our Jersey bedroom and felt a small space in the middle of my chest pop open and crackle with energy. As the day progressed, the energy spread more evenly through my chest and down towards my belly and turned into a uniform warmth that shot through my muscles. It was a kind of sexual tension I had never felt before, the kind that precedes the predator, the prey or the kill. It kept my pulse racing continuously in the anticipation of deliverance. But summer had come to an end and Alan had moved back to Philadelphia where he spent the non-summer months. I bided my time, knowing I would see Alan again.

His visits to Jersey City started casually at first – perhaps he had been in Princeton to visit his sister and wanted to drop in, or he was coming into the city for some business and thought he might pass through Jersey to say hello. He was always careful to visit when Yameen was there and brought something with him each time. Often he stayed back for Indian take-out and beer and crashed on our unsightly green couch. He was as gracious a guest as he was a host. He always left before we woke up, his blanket neatly folded into a square on one corner of the couch, the dirty dishes from the previous night washed and stacked by the sink. I counted the seconds till his next visit.

It was Alan who suggested that I assist him in his new job. He was always looking for new projects and finding them without much trouble. His latest project required him to haunt different bars and lounges in Manhattan and promote certain brands of liquor. Why he needed an assistant for a job as ridiculously easy as that, I need not have asked. I had to wear a yellow and red T-shirt with a tight black skirt, set up a table on one side of our chosen bar with sample items and drinks and then simply coax drunk men and women to try our free samples. After work, Alan and I put away our table of samples and danced the night away. In the early hours of dawn Alan would drop me home, where I slept till evening when it was time to be with him again.

While my mother complained incessantly about the inde- terminate quality of her life, trapped between her dreams and her destiny, I felt that my life had never been better than when it was in perfect limbo, between reality and fantasy. I was back in the pink bathroom of childhood, simultaneously performer and audience, and there was no incorrect move. The city now was no longer an apparition from my kitchen window. I roamed it freely in the dark, holding Alan's hand, slinking up to the unknown, attractive faces on the sidewalk and dance floor with complete ease. Yameen came to join us sometimes but he always left in a drunken daze halfway through the evening. Perhaps he felt left out. There was nothing I could do for him. He was the Heart-ravisher that I had created. And now that he had ravished my heart, and all the love in it, I had nothing else to give him. Often he barked at me, speech slurred, 'I know you, I know what you're doing! I've always known you!'

It wasn't until a few months had passed and I was heart-sick from the sexual longing between us that I realised just how religious Alan was. I caught whiffs of his religious sentiments when, in moments of weakness, he revealed his need for intimacy followed immediately by self-debasement. One day, after we kissed, he leaned back into the soft leathery coolness of the couch we were sitting on at a club called Cream and let out a long, meaningful sigh. Silver strobes of light from the dance floor zigzagged across his face and as I brought my still-warm lips closer to his mouth again, I caught the chill creeping into his features. 'What's wrong?' I asked, reaching for his hand.

'Nothing,' he said, tenderly pushing a strand of hair from my eyes, 'I was just thinking about marriage, how some people stay happily married for ever.'

Is that what you want?' I asked playfully, still unaware of the despondency behind his words, 'To be happily married?'

'I don't know,' he said, 'I had my chance with someone a long time ago and I blew it. But ideally, two people in love should be married, yes. That is the right way, the way God intended it to be.'

My heart twisted with wariness. The sweetness of the kiss had passed and I was left with the old, familiar feeling of being caught in an act of treason. Still, such moments were rare, at least in the beginning, and Alan's natural countenance was so much the opposite of judgmental that I found it hard to remember them afterwards. If he did manage to upset me with one of his views on good versus evil or sin versus virtue, he immediately compensated with an outpouring of apologies and assurance and loving embraces. If there was one thing that Alan did for me more than anyone ever has, it was the task of reading every single emotion that ever appeared on my face. He knew every smile, every look, every sigh, every turn of my head. He knew so much of me and about me and I so little about him. But I know that he fought with himself, with his innermost impulses, which, sadly, separated his passion from his piety.

I have no true way of guessing, even to this day, what drove Alan to make love to me for the first time. Perhaps he was unable to resist his desire even though he considered it sinful, or maybe he chose to be with me because that night, that one night, everything other than the two of us seemed truly irrelevant to him. Perhaps my disdain for religious rigor made it momentarily possible for him to overcome his own reservations. The God of my childhood was a punitive figure who hid amidst prayer mats and holy books and repetitive rituals and dispensed punishment at the slightest sign of non-compliance. But the God of my adult life was increasingly different, still only partially visible but gaining definition with time. This new God was more humorous, less masculine. This God had me placing a lonesome rose underneath my father's photograph on the anniversary of his death rather than visit his grave to pray for his soul. My mother didn't understand it, but this God did. This God had me smiling with gratitude when I found myself, finally, mercifully, in Alan's naked arms.

We parked his car around my block in the last hours of the night and undressed ourselves in the pallid pre-dawn light. We were hardly bothered by the cramped interior of the car or the faint comprehension that anyone looking in from outside might easily have seen our every move through the car's windows. The pleasure I felt was timeless, pronounced, exceptionally calming. I was twelve years old again, rubbing the sleep out of my eyes as Shonali dragged me and Naveen out of bed to join her for an early morning walk. Shonali insisted on those daily walks and her primary objective was to pick the fallen shiuli flowers along the silent alleys we passed, before the city came alive and trampled the tiny flowers to extinction. There was nothing sexually suggestive about those walks but something about the sight and scent of a shiuli, all creamy white petals and delicate orange stem, quietly releasing its sensuous perfume, heightened my senses and made my skin tingle.

That heady scent from long ago flooded my memory and filled my breath on that morning with Alan and it was the first time in my life that I saw myself through my own eyes while in the act of lovemaking – as curious and open as I had been on those shiuli-picking mornings. How dreamlike the world had seemed in those torpid hours, how mysterious the houses in our neighbourhood, how surreptitious yet inviting the shadowy lanes. And how ironic and yet how necessary that I should find that fragrance and that mystery again in the filthy streets of a strange foreign neighbourhood, in the arms of a lover I was not to have.

It was so much harder for Alan. His joy, though genuine, was somehow furtive, finite, as if he needed to return what he had only borrowed. What invigorated my faith in myself, in my ability to laugh and love, only depleted his confidence in himself, in us. Wide-eyed I watched myself come alive in Alan's presence but realised how he was unaware of the lasting imprint he left on me. I tried, for Alan's sake, to restrain my elation, to bring to our relationship the quality of suffering I knew would ease his torment. But I had little control over the person I was becoming. I had worked too hard and too long to contain myself. My mind now was disinclined to remain subdued, my body unobligingly demanding. Alas, what was my transformation was but a painful transgression for Alan. He went through different stages of guilt even as he succumbed to the experience.

'Doesn't it feel right at all?' I asked him when he buried his head in my lap and sobbed or moped for days.

'Of course it does,' he answered.

'Then why so guilty?'

'How can you be so simplistic? Feeling good is not the same as being good.'

But wasn't it? And why couldn't it be?

Unknowingly, Alan voiced what I had always feared. It was

the one fear I'd kept running from, the one true God who had ruled my being. But with Alan I was heedless of this God. For once, I had felt no need to run or deny or hide or prove or create or destroy. For once, something was just happening to me without censor or ceremony, without prospect or purpose, without shame or pride. It was too uncontainable to be friendship, too instinctive to be an adventure and too harmonious to be love. It begged to find its own way.

If only Alan could have done without answers. He came by in the afternoon sometimes when Yameen was at work but these visits were awkward, unsettling affairs unlike his buoyant, amicable visits from the early days. In broad daylight, he was careful not to touch me and jumped if my skin brushed against his by accident. It was almost impossible to imagine that a few hours later, sheathed by nightfall, loud noise and large crowds, Alan and I would be inseparable for most of the night. He would wrap his long arms around my waist and whisper to me his most private thoughts and I would feel his words stoke a fire somewhere deep inside me like they always did. I began to dread his daytime visits because I knew they were his attempts, however unconscious and hapless, to make sense of our love, to see if indeed it still felt like love without the mask of darkness. The hardest part was to try and answer his questions; questions that sounded valid but felt insubstantial. Was I happy with him? What did the future hold in store for us? And how could he live with himself? I stood facing him in the suffocating brown kitchen, distraught, diminished by his guilt. Mother's accusing eyes hovered above us, as if to say, Is this what I have taught you? After all that you have seen me suffer, is this the best you can do for yourself? Not knowing what else to do I followed the lead of her accusing eyes and reproved Alan for his weakness.

'You don't love me,' I retorted. 'If this was about love, your guilt would not have stood in the way.'

'How can you say that?' he pleaded. 'You know I love you. But you are married to my friend.'

'I didn't want to marry him.'

'But you did, didn't you?'

Much like a bystander, I watched Alan thrash about in his doubt and remorse. For the first time ever, I was free of those insidious elements, and despite my love for him, I did not want to reach out and soothe his sores, lest they rub off on me. The nights we worked together were infected with his growing affliction. He avoided my eyes, languished and sulked in my presence and went to great trouble to keep me at arm's length until, one day, I stopped going to work. It must have been what Alan had hoped for, because shortly thereafter, he stopped his visits to Thorne Street.

I hadn't seen him in weeks when he called me one night and I could tell he had been crying. 'I made a confession in church today. Then I called Yameen but he wouldn't talk to me,' he said.

'What do you want to tell Yameen?' I asked.

'That I'm sorry. So very sorry.'

'And you think that'll make it better?'

'I don't know. I have to try . . .' he couldn't finish his sentence.

Just like that, we had come to an end. Words had run out, love had receded and memories too would pale, no doubt. How I wished my first taste of love had not ended with an aftertaste of atonement, a petition for pardon.

'Good luck then,' I managed, unable to say goodbye.

At last, I was truly alone in that decrepit flat. I was barred from entering the bedroom where Yameen slept alone. During the day he locked the bedroom door and took the key with him to work. I moved my possessions into the guestroom, the only room in the apartment, which had been painted a canary yellow by Yameen's former flatmate. A real bed had finally been purchased for the bedroom, and with my shift to the guestroom I was forced, once again, to sleep on the rotting futon. I slept fitfully during the nights and, if I happened to wake before sunrise, my mind came undone in the darkness. I wished for the frigid draft pushing in through the window to turn into a warm midsummer night's breeze. I strained to hear the harsh cawing of tropical crows signalling daybreak. I could smell a rain-soaked Dhaka, spicy, earthy, beguiling in her freshness. The kodom tree at the entrance of our house would have bloomed by now, its musk extending beyond its shade. Shonali, devoted lover of flowers, used to pluck the bald-headed petalless flowers and stick them haphazardly in a vase in the centre of our living room. No one liked to look at the oddly shaped flowers but each one of us was drawn to the living room by their unique scent.

'This is why Krishna played his flute under the kodom tree,' Shonali told us gravely, running her fingers lightly above the spiky, egg-headed flowers. 'Because he too was ugly, like the kodom flower. But the sound of his flute, like the smell of kodom, was sweeter than life.' Inspired by her own sombre theory, she would break into a melancholy tune about Radha–Krishna's tragic love story.

I yearned for Shonali's wisdom on those lonely nights,

craved her callused fingers rubbing oil into my scalp and missed, terribly, her gruesome humour. I missed seeing the first sign of an approaching storm in the sudden and drastic disappearance of the sun, the earth's sublimation from a hot, diaphanous liquid into a cool, dark piece of chocolate. I missed Mother's insufferable presence, where I felt safe if not free. I missed the Big House and the herb-filled balcony of our smaller one. I missed oranges and spices and the cacophony of too many voices speaking at once. I missed even the ubiquitous God who had disciplined me as a child. Entrapped by the sickening yellow walls of a noiseless room, I missed being watched, followed, scrutinised. Never before had my adolescent years seemed so alive, so palpable and fiery as they did from where I lay, etherised, on that stinking mattress. What if my father were to ask me again to never leave Dhaka? What would I say to him this time? Would I stay? Or would I make again this long and arduous journey only to find that it was I and only I who was standing at the end of it?

The paraplegic man across the street is not in his usual place today. His chair sits barren, purposeless. In every other way, it is morning as usual on Thorne Street. From my position by the window, I see cars zooming by like flashes of lightning. The little Russian lady is tip-toeing her way into my herb garden, an attempted replica of Mother's work. Should I run downstairs and tell her that she need not sneak into my garden any more? Should I, perhaps, ask her if she would, from time to time, water my herbs so they may continue to live after I am gone?

Standing next to me, Yameen is drinking an opaque liquid

from a large mug. This is not the first time he has drunk in the morning hours but I have rarely seen him drink so fast. In his agitation, he consumes the strong-smelling liquid as if it were a life-saving remedy. A white truck pulls up at the kerb. I tell Yameen the movers are here.

'So you'll come back in a few months?' he asks dully.

'I'm taking all my things,' I reply gently.

'I'm not asking about your things, I'm asking about you.'

I remain silent.

'You told me you just need time to think,' he says, edging on despair.

'It is time to go,' I say.

Sluggishly, painstakingly Yameen plods back to the couch. He sits there, unmoving, eyes glistening, lips curling with the impending threat of tears. All those tears. I stare at Yameen and for a moment, I wonder if that's how my father had felt – waiting, helplessly waiting – for my mother to step into his world and into his heart. I stand paralysed, until one of the movers breaks the onerous moment.

'Are these boxes coming too?' he asks, pointing at Yameen's old boxes.

'No,' I say. 'Those will stay.'

Sweet, Sour and Bitter

Green and yellow patches of marshland glisten in the morning sun, giving way to narrow lanes winding around low white-washed tenements, that eventually merge into bigger and busier streets crawling with buses, trucks and the sheer mass of human bodies. All of this shrouded and trapped under a stagnant blue-grey cloud of smog. This is what I see as the aircraft begins its descent towards Zia International Airport. The woman next to me is furiously patting her chocolate-brown face with chalk-white powder as her husband tries to calm their small son. The little boy keeps trying to grab at his mother as she pulls one atrocity after another from her handbag to make herself presentable for the imminent reunion. She now slashes her lips with a deep maroon lipstick, the colour of clotted blood, and finishes off by slapping hot-pink blotches on her cheekbones. The aircraft makes a final swoop and the child begins to wail. As soon as the stewardess unlocks the cabin door a surge of heat brings with it a rush of smells: sweat, aerosol fumes, old leather and urine. As they hit my nostrils something in my gait changes involuntarily: a subtle shift in my posture, a familiar repositioning of the angle of my spine. I am readjusting, realigning, rearranging into my other self. I am in Dhaka.

I am back at my grandmother's house, the same house where I used to spend a few weeks of each summer as a young girl. The once-white walls are a jaundiced yellow, peeling, exposing large grey blocks of cement. I stroll through the front yard, pausing at the locked entrance of what we used to call the abandoned garden, inside which is a burnt-down shack, untended mangroves and stubborn weeds. There I had played for hours until my grandmother came to drag me back to the house, gasping at my arms and legs that had been bitten raw. Every day my grandmother warned me not to play in the abandoned garden, she told me the shack was haunted and spirits lived among the wild thickets. I went back again and again, in search of the poor spirits, waiting for them to hit my face like a gust of hot wind as my grandmother had described. 'I'm warning you, if that bad wind hits your face, you'll go insane,' she would caution. I wished.

I turn away from the locked entrance to what is no longer an enchanted garden but a tiny, pruned piece of land, wearily bearing a FOR SALE sign. At the very end of the frontyard I stop before the little corrugated tin shed. The door is ajar, I can hear voices inside. Someone lives here now? The rickety door of this cabin was boarded up and locked in previous years. I had never wondered what was behind that door.

My grandmother sits nonchalantly chewing her betel leaf and stirring sugar into her tea as if she has not heard my question. I ask her again, 'Who lived in that tin shed, Nanu?'

She pours some tea into the saucer, blows on it and laps it up. 'A man lived there', she says, 'a very long time ago.' She reaches under her bed and pulls out a gold brass spittoon layered with at least five generations of betel-juice spit. She holds it up to the light. 'This belonged to my mother, who got it from her mother . . .' Her voice trails off then picks up again, 'I never saw my father but I heard that he brought home hot mango pickle for my mother every evening because she always had a craving for it.'

My great-grandmother Mehrunessa married my great-grandfather Sohrab Hossain when she was thirteen and he was nineteen. She was seventeen years old and pregnant with their fourth child when he died of cholera. He went to the outhouse one evening and didn't return for two hours. When they found him, he was lying face down, unconscious and drenched in sweat. He died two days later. He was all she had. A hundred years ago, when my great-grandmother was a little girl, she was never allowed to leave the house to go to school or play outside. But Sohrab Hossain was her first cousin so she was allowed to talk to him. They spoke only through love letters. When he died, she lost her mind. She did not recognise her three children, refused to touch her food, screamed and kicked for hours and tried to run away several times. No one could talk reason into her so they decided to chain her to her bed. When one of her children tried to get close to her she would look away or stare blankly. Then she had a dream.

Mehrunessa had been sleeping chained to this very bed that my grandmother and I are sitting on. She had been sleeping with these very windows wide open as a storm was about to come. It woke her and she turned just in time to see that a cloud had descended all the way to the window next to her bed. Inside the cloud was a silver chariot carrying her husband. She sighed and reached for him with her hand-cuffed limbs. He stepped off the chariot but he did not take her hand. 'Listen to me,' he said firmly. 'Your time has not come. Have you forgotten that you are carrying our child and have three others to look after? When your time comes, I promise to come and get you.' She watched him leave, the chariot cloud disappearing into the grey horizon. The rain that had threatened to split the sky open just a few minutes earlier never came. Instead the clouds gave way to a hesitant sun.

Mehrunessa jerked upright in bed and looked around in wonder. A snot-nosed toddler was playing on the floor next to her bed. Hadn't anyone bathed her little daughter in days? She called out in a loud, incredulous voice, 'Why on earth am I chained? Are you all *crazy?*'

Mehrunessa was stuck in the classic dilemma of the middle-class widow. She had no inheritance but could neither seek work nor reconcile herself to the idea of remarriage. She lived on a dole, meted out by extended family members, keeping up the pretence of respectability but denying herself and her children every possible pleasure. It was during those years that Najib Ali came into their lives. Her sons needed a tutor and someone wisely suggested that the little tin storage shed could be easily rented out. That was how Najib Ali, a young student of English Literature at the local university, moved into the tin shed, among the piles of junk, in the role of tutor–tenant. The villagers speculated about the young man. There was a rumour that he had fled from his village because of an uncaring father and stepmother. Though he was often seen walking in the frontyard with a book of poetry, he hardly spoke at all. In the evenings, Mehrunessa sent a servant boy with a tray of warm food to the little tin shed. This could have gone on indefinitely, but here the story veers off into a million arteries, each carrying blood to the birth of an event whose truth or exact details no one really knows.

Did Najib Ali turn up at the main house one day, knock on the door and ask to see the lady of the house for a face-to-face introduction? Did the lady of the house invite him in for a glass of cool lemonade one lonely afternoon when the over-powering July sun made it impossible to have a siesta? Or perhaps the servant boy fell ill one day and my great-grand-mother decided to pull on her dark veil and carry the tray of food to Najib Ali herself. Perhaps, when he opened the door, he saw her shivering slightly, eyes shimmering in the dark. It's possible too that she ran up unveiled to the roof one windy day, rushing to collect the dry clothes before the rains came and, Najib Ali, not expecting to be discovered, had strolled up there to enjoy Keats under an open sky. Their eyes met, he saw her long hair snaking past her waist, she noticed his delicate fingers clutching the book to his heart. She lowered her eyes first but he couldn't look away.

Years later, Najib Ali showed no signs of returning to his own village, nor did he seem keen on securing another job, even though the boys had almost outgrown his tutelage. My grandmother who had been only five years old when he had arrived on their premises grew up to be an adolescent in his presence. He had become more than a tutor, he had become a permanent fixture. When Najib Ali's father came to visit him he was so impressed with the way his son's health and manner had improved that he went to Mehrunessa and said, 'My son is now under your care. I will not come to see him any more.'

At about the same time, vicious gossip started to spread. It had been almost eight years of cohabitation and companionship. Mehrunessa's reputation was the most important thing to her. Najib Ali could have left in the middle of the night or he could have stayed on as he was, defying scandal. It was not up to him. Mehrunessa locked herself in her room until she reached a decision.

Did my great-grandmother think it a tribute to her dead husband to prove her chastity to the world? Or did she feel that her children should not have to suffer the humiliation of an ill-reputed mother? I only know that after many sleepless nights, Mehrunessa decided that the only way to stop the wagging tongues and correct her slandered reputation was to have Najib Ali marry her thirteen-year-old daughter, my grandmother.

Najib Ali did not agree to this proposition. How could he marry a girl who had sat on his lap with her thumb in her mouth, a mere child? But when the insane streak flared in my great-grandmother, no amount of reasoning worked. I imagine she attacked him with her rapacious rage, hair flying, eyes flashing, consuming him completely with her anger and her beauty. I imagine Najib Ali realised that if he wanted to stay in the only place he had ever received love, he had no choice. Or, could it be that Mehrunessa did not want him to leave? And this was the only way she knew how to guarantee his presence in her life? Whatever they had shared was larger than them. To contain it, ordinary measures would not be enough.

Like her mother Mehrunessa, Saira was also married at thirteen. Saira had just had her first period but had still not outgrown her frocks when they adorned her in bridal garments and told her she was now the wife of Najib Ali. Saira did not protest. She thought it was fun to dress up in beautiful clothes and jewellery, never doubting that she would return to school and her dolls after the festivities ended. Not too late in the wedding night, the bride went missing. Mehrunessa found her daughter fast asleep in her own bed, still dressed like a bride. It took the older women of her family much time to convince Saira to start sleeping in her husband's bed.

Najib Ali moved into the main bedroom of the main house, while Mehrunessa moved to a smaller guest chamber. Every night, Saira, exhausted from demanding that she be allowed to go to school or to the playfield, climbed back into her own bed and fell into a confused sleep. Many nights, her mother or her aunt would carry her sleeping form to her husband's bed but she would always find her way back. Not knowing what else to do, the women implored upon Najib Ali to take a stronger stand. Keep her in bed! Act like a husband! A month later, both Saira and Najib Ali succumbed to their fates and Saira soon became pregnant with her first child.

My grandmother stops speaking, reaches for the gold filigreed spittoon and spurts a glob of red juice into it. 'So, there you are,' she sighs, 'it was your grandfather who lived in that tin shed.'

My grandfather. The stranger. The poet. The teacher. The friend. The dutiful husband. But what kind of a lover was he?

'Did you love him?' I ask Nanu.

Nanu doesn't answer. A wind howls around the crumbling cottage, pushing past the wooden traps of the old windows.

We hear the sky rumble, followed by the thuds of tree-ripened mangoes in the backyard. The scents of monsoon flowers – keya and champa – rise up from somewhere. By the big pond behind the house, a bunch of naked slum children shriek in anticipation of the swiftly approaching torrent. I wait uncertainly, in the pale blue light, but Nanu is somewhere far away.

The year before, Alan had visited Nanu's cottage. True to his wish, he had accompanied Yameen and me to Dhaka to see the places of my youth. He had looked cartoon-like in my great-grandmother's ancient mahogany four-poster bed, his long body curled in a defensively shy manner, blue eyes scouting the unfamiliar terrain. Is that how I had looked to him one summer in Amagansett, childlike, ready to recoil at the first sign of trouble in an unusual world? Or had I been too inviting, too eager for transformation?

I took Alan and Yameen to see the smoky mountains of Sylhet along with the rest of my family. We rented a quaint bungalow on a tea estate, surrounded by acres of garden. In the evenings we played card games around a fire. Sometimes, when I peered at the darkness beyond the windows invaded only by the flicker of a firefly, I let myself imagine I was back in Bagh Bari and Father was in the next room, reading his newspaper. Deer skins and stuffed tiger heads, not unlike the ones in my paternal grandfather's house, hung above us in watchful silence. The mornings were more lucid, leaving less room for imagination. Yameen wandered off on his own, hauling his tripod on his shoulders. I knew that the photographs he took would end up in one of the brown cardboard boxes in his bedroom, next to thousands of other pictures he had taken during his travels. With his numerous

cameras he tried to capture and freeze a beauty that escaped
the normal lens of his vision. In my presence he maintained
a reproachful distance, never asking for anything, as if to say
that he had no interest in the world that he suspected would
reclaim me into its depths. But every once in a while he
emerged from his sullenness and made a feeble attempt to
make himself known. 'Interesting place,' he'd say, 'but I can't
see you here any more.' Need I tell him that he didn't see me
at all?

Though I had never hoped for the fervour of our time
together in Amagansett or New York, a part of me was startled by the aloofness with which Alan regarded me while in
Bangladesh, the place he had been so eager to share with me.
I played the polite host and he was the gracious guest, as we
had been during his first visits to Thorne Street. Yet he got
along superbly with my mother. Just as Alan had guessed, it
was as if they had always known each other. My mother
couldn't imagine why a wonderful man like Alan was not
married with children. That, to her, was even more perplex-
ing than my own shabby attempt at domesticity. One
morning I woke up to find Alan sitting in the garden staring
into the distance. From the way he held his body, arched and
beseeching, I knew he was deep in prayer. I watched him for
a few minutes then called out his name. He turned quickly,
and for a minute I saw in his sunken eyes the dead weight of
remorse. Seeing Alan like that broke me in much the same
way as loving him had kept me together – quietly,
irreversibly.

On our last day in Sylhet Alan approached me on the open
balcony where I was watching the afternoon diffuse into a

purple twilight. Avi and Yameen had gone into town and Mother and Naveen were resting in their rooms.

'I wanted to thank you,' he said, smiling sadly.

'What for?' I tried to smile back.

'I've been meaning to tell you that this place is full of magic. I've never been anywhere like this and I've never been so inspired to pray.'

'What did you pray for?' I ask, knowing that he wanted me to.

'I prayed for you,' he said, unhesitatingly, 'I prayed for us to find happiness.'

I stared at him. Had he really not known? Had he not felt the pure joy when we were together in the candle-lit rooms of Amagansett, that flickering light a deceptive testament to the raging fire in our hearts. What else was needed to give happiness its legitimate credit? What blessing was required, and in which God's name, to turn shame into love and grief into bliss? And what of those who never find themselves face to face with God? Does their love amount to nothing? Are they forever suspended between love and its sanctification? But I began to understand, truly, why Alan was so drawn to my history, my life. He perceived, somewhere in its tangle, his own piteous need to be judged, punished and finally forgiven, before he could feel free to pursue his own. And it dawned on me why Mother and Alan were so fond of each other.

The storm has subsided and the rain now comes at a slower, steadier pace. The blue light around us begins to clear. Nanu shifts her position. She reaches for the spittoon one more time, spits into it and clears her throat.

'Your Nana wanted me to chew paan. He liked the way it always kept my lips red.'

'He must have been smitten by you,' I tease her.

She reddens. She has already shared too much. Never, not once, other than that monsoon's day, have I heard my grandmother talk about love or pleasure or anguish. She has lived all of it, from the red in her lips to the grey around her temples, even if she cannot put any of it into words. But I haven't inherited Mehrunessa's gall or Saira's grace or even my mother's charm. I have inherited only the tender cores of their spirits – famished for love, for redemption, for exaltation. It erupts from my centre, this hankering for love, this lava-like substance, both cleansing and noxious, heating my body and cooling my soul, constantly shifting the tectonic plates of my existence.

Had my great-grandmother truly felt redeemed after she had proved the absolution of her love for Sohrab Hossain? Was my grandmother so cryptic in her revelations of conjugal love because she had never even grasped its essence? And was my mother, perpetually starved for something or another, the perfect example of a woman wanting of love?

Up and down we bounce, from one love to another. From the flowing, unconditional sustenance of the amniotic waters to the toughening, challenging love of our fathers to the warm, unburdening love of siblings to the bittersweet love of a lover to the indescribable love for our children to the untenable love of ambition to the exhausting love for our work to the unfathomable love of God. But where are *we* in all this? Where is the *I* in the *you* and *me*?

If I think back to the origin of the feeling, I see that my eagerness has always trumped the experience. One of the first and most frequently repeated stories I heard from my mother was about her miraculous ability to incite love in the heart of whoever happened to lay eyes on her. The love letters started pouring in from the time she was thirteen. Anonymous notes were tucked into her schoolbag, some were pressed into her startled hands and, every once in a while, one happened to fly in through an open window, tied to a stone. Whatever the method of delivery and whoever the writer, the letters carried the same content. They were endless monologues on her beauty, on the helpless nature of the letter-writer's feelings and on the undying hope of being united to the object of their love. Mother grew up, fattened by the richness of unbidden admiration. Even as a young girl, with no real knowledge of the opposite sex, she lived the victories of a desirable woman wielding her power over men. Without ever asking for it, she found, constantly, the one assurance we all need once we are out of the nursery and out of our mother's all-encompassing arms – the assurance that we are, indeed, worthy of someone else's love, the assurance that we may share with someone else the unparalleled sense of oneness that only a mother and infant share. But infancy is as much a curse as it is a blessing. We start life with the notion that our mothers will for ever preempt our falls, wake up to our cries and rock us into oblivion. For someone like my mother, who found a loving embrace never that far from reach, no matter how old or young she was, it must have been both easier and harder to cope. Easier when she basked in others' adoration and drew from it the strength and confidence she needed to come into her own. Harder when she expected others to forever cushion her falls far beyond her infant years. Either way, Mother was spared a free fall. She stumbled and rose, stumbled and rose.

I, on the other hand, tumbled out of the sweetness of my mother's arms and into the panic of my being in one fluid motion. As soon as I learned to understand her language, I knew that Mother was bidding me farewell, setting me on the stage of the world to play my part. You're no longer a child, she repeated like a mantra. Can't you grow up faster! When will I ever be free of you? I've done my dues – what else do you want from me? It unhinged my mother to think that she was to dole out affection rather than reel it in. She saw herself, forever young and exquisite in the love letters of her girlhood, while her children's raucous demands for her love left her anxious, gasping for breath.

I wonder now if my mother had sought from her music the same satisfying flattery that she was used to receiving from her admirers. She wanted music to make her famous, to give her the recognition and praise that so sustained her. But what was she to give to music? When was she to prove to music her love and devotion? Flabbergasted by the changing currents of fate that turned her from being the sought to the seeker, my mother declared herself to be a martyr. At least in her martyr-dom, she could still see herself being pursued by woe, by cruel gods who conspired to bring her misery. Oddly, it was her self-imposed martyrdom that finally brought her the courage she needed to shed some of her self-pity.

'I don't care any more what anyone says,' she says bitterly these days, 'I'm going to do whatever I want.'

'As you should,' I say.

'Oh I will,' she threatens.

And she does. She changes the upholstery of the living-room furniture into a bold zebra print and replaces the off-white curtains with sheer gold ones. She paints her room a luminous lavender and makes a resolute attempt to keep her matching bedspread smooth and unruffled. The dining room is slathered in vivid yellow and a red and green batik print of a humongous lobster is placed on the wall. But when she stands back to survey the changes, the zebra print seems too busy, the gold curtains are too transparent, the lavender in her room is suddenly more pink than purple and the dining room looks like a giant lemon about to be consumed by a monster bug. My mother is puzzled.

'Go for lighter tones,' I suggest.

'It's not the colours, silly,' she says, recovering her pride. 'It's the light in the rooms. The architecture of this flat is all wrong. It's not like the Big House.'

I remind her that the light comes in from the same direction for both the Big House and our flat.

'Oh, who cares about the light,' she waves me away. 'If I had the right amount of money to spend on this flat, then I could really do what needs to be done.'

'Then do it slowly, room by room,' I persist.

'Oh, to hell with it,' she cries. 'The kitchen is beyond redemption. The bathrooms need complete makeovers. I don't care any more!' Her voice is starting to quiver, she is losing her composure.

'What you've done isn't so bad,' I try to assure her.

'It doesn't matter. It's your time now. You're young and life awaits you. You should be doing all this, not me.' Her eyes flash and the curve of her neck is tense.

Why is Mother not as relieved as I had always expected her to be now that she is on her own? In her quest for freedom had she completely missed its shape-shifter spirit? Had she worked towards a vision which, upon closer look, was the opposite of freedom?

And is it only now that I see the martyr I have become, setting myself up for sacrifice, again and again, at the altar of music, of dance, of love? If I never could hold on to love, or the things I loved, it was only because I was too impatient to snatch at what I thought I needed, too keen to create for myself the ideal scenario. The sweetness of the experience eluded me because I was too busy apprehending its outcome. Just as my mother can never be free of her compulsion for freedom, I could never perfect my image of perfection.

Mother goes shopping again for materials. She sifts through the myriad of colours, never finding exactly what she needs but never admitting that no matter what she picks, it always seems to be a different shade of the same colour. Finally, tired of refurbishing and redecorating, Mother wants to sell the very property on which our home stands. It is not the loss of the land but the thought of demolishing the Big House that turns the conversation sour between us. Though we both know that we will never live in the Big House as a family, the mere fact that it is there, solid space that encases the vision of a beloved home, provides more comfort than I had ever admitted. At moments like this, I am confronted by the fragility of my life, its futility. On and on we dream, we wish, we love – no matter that the dreams come to an end, the wishes evolve or that love dissipates like dust in the wind. Perhaps, what matters only is that we have lived long enough to dream, hard enough to wish and indisputably enough to love.

* * *

185

Tonight I stand before a picture of myself in my mother's arms. I am a month old in the picture. My mother holds me up for the camera as I open my mouth in a broad, toothless grin. She peers from behind my infant body, proud and happy. Through the black and white of the picture I can almost discern the rosy glow spreading across her cheeks. I can feel my own body relaxing into the protective grip of her hands. I can sense the tight embrace that will reclaim me after the camera has flashed, the hot kisses that will cover my little face, the soft baby talk she will coo into my ears when she cradles me to sleep. Then I see it – the two long tears forming a lopsided cross upon the picture's surface. Someone had cleanly ripped the photograph into several pieces, which were now glued back in place.

'Who did this?' I ask my mother, outraged.

'You did. Don't you remember?' she says, as if I ask a rhetorical question.

'But why?' I am surprised because I have no memory of it.

'I don't know. You were upset about something, I presume.'

Had she never asked me why I was angry or did she just refrain from mentioning it now, lest she unleash some unpleasant memory between us? I lie awake trying to recall why I had torn the photograph and it finally comes to me. I was furious to find out that this was the only baby picture of myself with my mother. The next picture of me was on my second birthday and the one after that when I was five years old, both of which were group pictures. It was as if no one cared to capture my childish feats but dutifully recorded a few nondescript pictures of a family around a cake or siblings playing together. They were hazy long shots, where I deciphered neither the expressions on my face nor the language of my body. And my mother? She was nowhere near me.

I looked through the old family albums again and again. Countless pictures of my brother and sisters stared back as I frantically searched for ones of me. There were thoughtfully arranged pictures of Naveen at various ages, sitting naked in a baby tub, crawling, and learning to pose with her Bugs Bunny. There was Tilat, a moon-faced baby, traced through the years as she grew into a slim, beautiful child. And there was Avi, the apple of all our eyes, giggling from babyhood to adolescence with characteristic joyfulness. I was not there, not even as a shadow in the peripheral vision of the camera, not until I was much older and had learned to nimbly wedge myself into the shots. In jealous rage, I had picked up the singular black and white infant photograph of myself and tore it into three pieces. I wanted to destroy the one image that offensively alluded to all the other unrecorded ones.

But today, my eyes widen in surprise as I begin to notice something else. How had I missed the fine and careful effort with which the torn pieces had been glued back in place? Someone had put the pieces back together with delicate precision. The work of those fingers belied a purpose far beyond the immediacy of the task. Even the glue had not left any marks in the white back of the photograph. The cross that now remains across the picture's front is just a faint mark, like a long strand of dust waiting to be blown away. How could I have failed to see this labour of love?

And how could I have missed my mother's laughter all these years? A sweet, rumbling sound fills the room when she laughs. Did she not laugh as much when we were young? I remember her frustration only too well. Creasing her forehead in horizontal lines of consternation, she always regarded the four of us in terms of all the work that needed to be done rather than all the work she had already accomplished. Mother was not a slacker, but the idea of work tired her as much as the work itself, leaving her prematurely exhausted.

'What am I going to do with you kids? I don't know how to raise you into proper human beings!' she lamented to no one in particular. She'd groan and grumble about how old and withered she was going to be by the time we grew up and went our own ways. On the best of days, mother regarded her burden with a touch of self-satisfying irony. 'At least I should not want of care in my old age, after raising the four of you.'

There were also the fits of rage that left her breathless. I remember watching her from a distance, her body quivering, sweat glistening above her lips and on her brow. During such fits she constantly moved things within her reach, without really noticing them. Once when she had a fight with my father at the dinner table, she snatched my plate away just as I was about to bite into a gravy-covered potato. Another time she absently tore up an important school notice that Naveen had left on the coffee table.

In her wrath, Mother plucked the leaves of potted plants, poured half-finished tea out of still-hot cups and turned off the television in mid-show. It was as if by reconfiguring the world of matter around her she could redirect her inner energies. And when she yelled she did so with great intention, using the force of her voice rather than words. She wanted to convince the world with the sound of her pain rather than an explanation of it. She expected us to prostrate before her anger and concede that there was no reason to question her.

Even in those circumstances I was drawn to her, awed by the strength that drove her, commanded by her expectation to be loved and obeyed despite her unbecoming attributes. In no less part was I lured by the unsavoury promises of adulthood. I wanted to master that kind of crude command over those around me. In a way, I began to appreciate how I was always being told 'You will' and 'You must'. Clearly, I was seduced by the darker side of things and for this I fault no one.

Because, for all the fires I recall my mother lighting in her younger years, I also recall when my mother conducted herself with perfect grace. A few months after I married Yameen and moved back to America, she came to visit me. In the late afternoons I sat at the kitchen table and read while my mother cooked dinner. On one such occasion, she was frying butterfish with red onions and garlic, absently humming under her breath. The aroma of spicy fish coupled with her gentle humming transported me to another time when I used to perch at our dining table with my schoolbooks, listening to Amol singing above the sizzle of the frying pan. My father sat at the other end of the table, poring over his work, a glass of single malt by his side. From Naveen's room floated the faint notes of Chris de Burgh's 'Fatal Hesitation'. Every time our favourite lines in the song came up, Naveen and I chorused to them together, she from her room and I from the dining room. Father would raise his head for a second and then look back down at his yellow notepad. I realised, suddenly, that this sequence of events were repeated evening after evening, but Mother had always been missing from the routine. Where had she been?

I raised my eyes to look straight into my mother's. Mine were searching, hers reaching out. I'm right here, her light-brown eyes seemed to say. I saw her then, a woman alight but not burning, absent but not quite gone, demanding but only of those she loved.

A few weeks later, after my mother left, I opened the kitchen cabinet to grab the coffee jar and found a blue sticky note pasted on the inside of the cabinet door. It said:

You are the best of all
  Always remember that

I think my mother meant to say 'You're the best', in a casual American way, but by attaching the last two words – 'of all' – to her first sentence, she belied her recently acquired Americanism and confirmed her instinctive capacity to leave her own, loving, inimitable mark. For all the times you burn her to the ground, she will rise from the ashes. For all the times you chase her shadow, she will reveal her light to you so generously that you may live in the aftermath of its bright-ness. For all the times you wait for her to see you, she will turn to catch you at an odd second, when you stand with your heart exposed, unprepared for her kindness. That is my mother and, just like love, she is best preserved if you let go of her.

As I tuck her note into the kitchen drawer it dawns on me that it was only natural that Mother was missing from our customary evening ritual. If she had been there, 'Fatal Hesitation' would never have made as much sense as did it to Naveen and me back then and for the rest of our lives. It was all there in the words of the song, which we knew by heart.

To this day, when I thrum the tune of 'Fatal Hesitation', the lyrics form themselves into the image of a woman, lost and lonesome. She is walking barefoot on white sand, along a stretch of blue-green ocean, foamy frolicky waves teasing her toes. But every time she comes closer and I try to catch a glimpse of her, she looks away and all I can see is the curvaceous outline of her face, fanned by long, windswept hair. And though I can never see her face fully, I know exactly what she looks like.

I find myself increasingly drawn to babies, buttery masses of flesh and soft folds, unquenchable wells of thirst and desire from the moment they are born. Love, love, love, is all they ever want. Mouths agape, fists balled, their curled toes flail the air for more love. I think of my frail mother, manhandled by sixteen limbs, and I cannot resist smiling at her youthful consternation.

'You need to have a child,' Mother reminds me frequently nowadays.

'Why? You certainly never wanted to.'

'What do you mean by that?' she laughs nervously, not quite poised for a fight.

'Didn't you always say so?'

'I did not.'

'But you did!' I cry.

'What are you saying, exactly?'

'I'm just wondering if having a child is worth the trouble,' I say.

She bristles with irritation, her jaw tightens. This is when she will say exactly what she means not to say.

'This is just the kind of nonsense one has to deal with as a mother—' she stops short, checking herself in time.

'Don't worry, Mother. I might have a child if I find the right man.'

'Ha! There are millions of men, just pick the right one.'

I don't know what Mother guesses from such flippant discussions, but sometimes I do dream of being a mother. The age-old cycle will start again in me, filling my veins and organs with the promise of new life and love. We will play, my child and I, a new game of give and take, speaking a new language of right and wrong; we will laugh and cry, we will hug and part, we will doubt and share, but at the end of it all we will ask each other the same question that separates and unites us: Do you love me? Was it worth it then, the push and pull, the sweetness and the bitterness, the inevitable descent from womb to breast to lap to hard, unyielding ground?

Dhaka afternoons are as warm and tumescent as ripe gold olives. The tropical sun roasts the city and its dwellers into a caramel exhaustion. The rickshaw pullers lean against their parked vehicles, salt crystals gleaming on their strong brown backs. The crows flutter about impatiently, searching for food droppings. Young mothers in colourful saris throng the school gates as the last bell rings and children stream out, uniformed armies with heaving backpacks, faces alight with the arrival of freedom. The street children or tokai make a final push to sell their remaining merchandise of popcorn, balloons and flowers, before scampering off to roadside dhabas for the afternoon meal, stray dogs following at their heels.

At home, Amol rushes to perform the alchemical ritual of

lunch, slicing the afternoon air with the six most reassuring smells of my life – onions, garlic, ginger, turmeric, chilli and coriander. I kick off my school shoes and enter the kitchen. I tug at my mother's sari as she bends over the stove, making my presence known, taking in the smell of her coconut shampoo and soap. Naveen pokes her head in next, Tilat and Avi follow and soon there are too many of us in the small kitchen. Carrots are jabbed, greedy fingers dip into curries, drumsticks jump out of a pot. 'Get out of here!' Amol swats at us like flies but we swarm around him, buzzing with demands. My mother laughs. 'They're hungry,' she says tenderly.

We were hungry, but not just for food. We were hungry too for the delicious stretch of afternoon that spread before us, those gold-green hours of secrecy and silence that broke up the day into three essential parts, leaving the middle part for all things magical. In the dreamy olive shade of those afternoons, unburdened of morning's duties and unoccupied by evening's demands, each of us went our separate ways. In those sumptuously private hours, we found our own meandering paths to love, suffered our shames, lived our fears and forged our faiths.

But what made the afternoons perfect was the knowledge that at the end of our romps and gambols through those pre-twilight hours, we would come together again in a fire-flied dusk, to reconvene in the same, singular act of loving and living, together, as one entity.

Epilogue

On a cool September dawn, I awake to the promise of a new beginning. I am getting married a second time, three years after the end of my first marriage. I wake from a dreamless sleep and greet the brisk summer morning. I see the women who have come to scrub and polish me with their selection of unguents and bathe me in boiling hot water but I turn away from them. I will not allow them to paint my face into a glittering mask of red and gold. Luxuriously, I lather myself with Mother's coconut soap, letting the cool water wash away yesterday's scents. Standing before my mirror, I tuck fresh jasmines into my own hair, place a red bindi in the centre of my eyebrows and carefully smudge kajal under my eyelids. After I finish, I linger by the mirror, studying my reflection. I am looking for signs of fear, for shreds of doubt. The woman who stares back at me is neither apprehensive nor giddy. Calm and expectant, she basks in the lucidity of this moment. I open the door and let everyone in.

*   *   *

'Answer each question loudly and clearly,' says the kazi, stroking his grey stringy beard.

'Are you at least eighteen years of age?'

'I am.'

'Do you accept this Nikah which is sanctioned by law and deemed holy in the eyes of God?'

'Yes.'

'Miss, I cannot hear you. Speak louder.'

'Yes, I do.'

'Do you accept Asif Ahmed as your lawfully wedded husband?'

I close my eyes.

'Miss, would you answer the question?'

'Yes, yes I do.'

'Do you have any other reservations at this time?'

'I do not.'

'Then please repeat the word kobul three times to indicate your consent.'

'Kobul, kobul, kobul.'

'Will the witness please come forward to sign the Nikahanama?'

My grandmother's older brother steps forward.

'What is your name, sir?'

'Saidul Hossain.'

'And the name of your father, sir?

'I am the son of late Sohrab Hossain of Old Maulvi Bari, Comilla.'

'Please write your name and your father's name here,' the kazi points to a section of the marriage certificate.

At the sound of my great-grandfather's name, I raise my

veiled head. Before me I see my great-grandmother, mad, shackled to her bed, her face turned towards the majestic image of a chariot-cloud floating up to her window, carrying her husband Sohrab Hossain inside. He speaks to her his last words, words of hope that will last her a lifetime without him. He has come back now to speak his last words to me. He will always come back to witness these moments of love in the lives of his descendants. I sense him around me, gently reminding me that love hasn't disappeared, that it never does, that it only changes form. Old loves transmute themselves into new trust and new desires.

I see my great-grandmother on her daughter's wedding day. With her bony hands she wraps a red silk sari around my grandmother as she tells her, ever so softly, to be kind and loving to Najib Ali, who is now her husband. My grandmother looks up at her mother's face and sees only love in her eyes.

Now I see my grandmother on my mother's wedding day. She wipes the sweat off her brow as she enters the room where my mother is sitting, surrounded by a group of women. My mother looks resplendent in red and gold. Nanu approaches her with a small earthen bowl of orange turmeric paste. She dips her index finger in the bowl and touches the cool paste to her daughter's forehead. Turmeric, the ancient healer of all ailments, the antidote to decay and nature's generous source of beauty, given by mother to daughter as a token of love, as purifying and invigorating as turmeric itself.

I turn my head and search the crowded room. I see my mother, sitting in one corner, quiet and unmoving. Her spine is straight, her head slightly bent, her eyes are closed, her hands cupped before her face in a gesture of pleading. She is saying a prayer for me. I can feel her appeal to the universe to hold me tight and keep me safe. I can hear the rhythm of her heart, as if I were a child inside her womb again, tied to her forever.

Acknowledgements

I want to thank my teacher Rebecca Brown, for guiding me with such love when I first conceived this book. She never lost faith in my vision and never failed to make me feel special as I shared the pages with her. My heartfelt thanks to Kazi Anis Ahmed for pushing me beyond my comfort zone, for cheering me on, for answering all kinds of questions and for being such an invaluable friend over the years. I am truly grateful to Masud Khan Shujon for being unduly generous with his time and for providing me with so much insight when I really needed it. And last, but not least, I cannot find the words to thank my editor Diya Kar Hazra, who, with her kindness, patience and unbelievable warmth and clarity, helped this work come to fruition.

A Note on the Author

Maria Chaudhuri was born and raised in Bangladesh. She has a Bachelor of Arts in Philosophy and Religion from Mount Holyoke College, Massachusetts, and an MFA in Creative Writing from Goddard College, Vermont. Maria Chaudhuri's essays, features and short stories have been published in various collections, journals and literary magazines. She lives in Hong Kong.